INTEGRATED TURFgrass

Management for the Northern Great Plains

Edited by
Frederick P. Baxendale, Ph.D.
Roch E. Gaussoin, Ph.D.

Published in 1997, reprinted in 2004, 2006
University of Nebraska–Lincoln Extension
Institute of Agriculture and Natural Resources

MW01200334

Acknowledgments

The authors gratefully acknowledge the support of:

- Communications and Information Technology and Terry Meisenbach, Publications Coordinator, for support.

- The Nebraska Turfgrass Foundation for financial support.

- Research, Extension and teaching colleagues on the Turfgrass Science Team.

- Jim Kalish, Extension Entomology Technologist, for developing graphics.

- The O.M. Scott and Sons Company for providing art work and weed descriptions.

Table of Contents

Tables

Figures

Color Photos

Foreword

We are pleased to bring you this handbook, *Integrated Turfgrass Management for the Northern Great Plains.* It was written by Extension faculty and researchers and co-edited by Drs. Fred Baxendale, Extension Entomologist, and Roch Gaussoin, Extension Turfgrass Specialist, of the University of Nebraska. Each author has drawn upon research results in addition to years of experience. We believe this handbook will be a useful tool and highly valuable to turfgrass professionals and to those interested in developing and maintaining a high quality turf.

Turfgrasses continue to increase in importance in Nebraska, the Northern Great Plains, and the nation as a whole. With the importance of our leisure time, the increasing popularity of golf, and the concern for improving the quality of our environment, turfgrasses will continue to increase in their significance. Good turfgrasses enhance the quality of our lives.

All too often, people assume that high quality turfgrasses just occur. Nothing could be further from the fact. High quality turfgrasses are like any other commodity in that they require careful attention and good management.

The values of American society are changing to place more emphasis on one's environment at work, at home, and during leisure activities. Psychologists continue to remind us of how important one's environment is to creativity and productivity during both our work and play. It is in this context that we believe this handbook will be highly beneficial to a growing and productive society.

The University of Nebraska is proud of its turfgrass program. We have many outstanding faculty, staff, and students associated with this effort. Although the University has had a turfgrass program for many years, it has grown significantly in size and stature during the last two decades and has now developed into a Center of Excellence for our University.

Dr. Martin A. Massengale
Director, Center for Grassland Studies

Integrated Turfgrass Management

Roch E. Gaussoin
Extension Turfgrass Specialist
with Jim Hruskoci
Extension Educator, Hall County
Donald Steinegger
Extension Ornamental Specialist

- Establishment
- Renovation
- Fertilization
- Irrigation
- Soil cultivation
- Thatch
- Pesticides

Turfgrass is an integral component of the landscape and is essential to quality sports turfs. Turfgrasses prevent soil erosion and reduce heat, noise, and glare. Several cultural practices are needed to maintain a healthy turf. The level at which these practices are implemented affects the turf's vigor and appearance.

Integrated pest management (IPM) promotes the use of more than one approach to keep pest populations at acceptable levels. The turfgrass IPM approach uses adapted grasses and cultural practices to prevent or reduce pest problems. The goal is to reduce pesticide use and dependency on pesticides. An IPM approach does not eliminate pesticide use because there may be cases when it is warranted. When pesticides are needed, select the safest, most effective chemical available, and follow specific label directions.

This section covers basic cultural practices of turfgrass management. Each cultural practice should be considered an interactive component of the total management system. Interactions of these components determine the level of success.

Turfgrasses

Turfgrass species can be divided into two major groups: cool season and warm season. Grasses vary depending on their soil temperature growth range.

Cool season turfgrasses are the most widely used in the Northern Great Plains. They include Kentucky bluegrass, tall fescue, perennial ryegrass, fine fescues, and bentgrass. Cool season grasses grow best when soil temperatures are 60°F-70°F. They grow most actively in the spring and fall, with growth slowing during summer. Cool season turfgrass species vary in adaptation, texture, color, and maintenance require-ments. Most cool season grasses are established by seed or sod. Proper species and cultivar selection are keys to improved turf performance.

Warm season turfgrasses, like zoysiagrass, bermuda-grass, and buffalograss, grow best when soil temperatures are 80°F-90°F. Warm season grasses are more heat and drought tolerant and more wear resistant than cool season grasses, but are gener-ally less tolerant to low temperatures. Warm season grasses remain dormant late in the spring, grow most actively during the warm summer, and become dormant with the first fall frost. Most warm season turfgrasses are established by sod plugs or sprigs (stolons). Buffalograss and blue grama are exceptions, being established commonly from seed. Characteristics of grasses grown in the Northern Great Plains can be seen in *Table 8*.

Establishment and Renovation

by Jim Hruskoci,
Extension Educator,
Hall County, Grand Island

Turfgrasses can be established from seed or vegetatively propagated using sod, sprigs, or plugs. Establishment method will depend on species, availability, and economics. The basics of establishment for cool and warm season grasses are identical except for timing. Cool season grasses are best established in the late summer or early fall; whereas warm season grasses are best installed in late spring or early summer. Proper site preparation is critical to the long-term success of a turf and its perpetual management.

New Turf Installations

The initial steps in turfgrass establishment are:

1. Test the soil
2. Control weeds
3. Establish rough grade
4. Add soil amendments
5. Establish final grade
6. Apply seed, sprigs, plugs, or sod
7. Rake or roll
8. Irrigate
9. Mow

Soil Test. At the very minimum an initial soil test should include phosphorous and potassium content and soil pH. See page 10 in the fertilization section of this chapter for proper sampling technique.

Weed Control. Weed populations can be significantly reduced if proper steps are taken during establishment. Prior to seeding, an irrigation, followed by a light, mechanical cultivation can alleviate the weed pressure that is prevalent in a new seeding. This approach is more successful on annual weeds than perennial weeds. For perennial weeds replace the mechanical cultivation with an application of a systemic, non-selective herbicide. A final, much more aggressive approach is sterilization of the area prior to seeding. Sterilization, when done properly, controls weeds as well as soil borne plant pathogens and insects. Sterilization is, however, relatively expensive and normally requires that certified applicators apply the sterilant.

3

Rough Grade Establishment. Fill in low spots and level undesired elevated spots. Contour grade relative to landscape design specifications. Install drainage if required. If rough grading is extensive, remove and stockpile topsoil for use in final grade establishment. If existing large trees are to be used in the final landscape, avoid adding or removing more than two inches of soil. If extensive excavation is to be done around a tree, consider using a tree well or removing the tree with a tree spade and replanting after establishment of rough grade.

Soil amendments. After establishing the rough grade the site is ready for any required or desired soil amendments. The pH of the soil (obtained from the soil test) may indicate the need for lime or sulfur as a soil amendment. In general, apply lime if your soil pH is below 5.5. If above 7.5, sulfur may be required to lower soil pH. This is also the ideal time to apply a "starter fertilizer". Starter fertilizers normally contain nutrients in a ratio of 1:1:1 and are important in the successful establishment of new turfgrass plantings. Some starter fertilizers will also contain siduron, a preemergence herbicide to inhibit grassy weed competition in the seed bed. Use fertilizers containing siduron for spring seedings.

Final Grade Establishment. Final grading should be done immediately prior to seeding, sodding or sprigging. Remove rocks or other debris which surfaced during grading. Rake or drag the area with a piece of chain-link fence or wooden drag for final smoothing.

Applying seed, sprigs, plugs, or sod. The choice of whether to use seed or vegetative material depends on many factors. Establishment from seed is the least expensive method, but it is also the slowest and most labor intensive post-planting.

Sodding is the most expensive initially, but establishment time is greatly diminished compared to seeding, and subsequent management during the establishment year is greatly reduced. Sprigging and plugging, depending on species, fall between seeding and sodding in terms of cost and initial management intensity. Make sure you use a high quality certified planting material.

If using seed be sure the seed is "certified," which is usually indicated by a blue tag on the seed bag. Depending on your state, sod also may be certified. Check with the Crop Improvement Office in your state for a list of certified sod growers. Many sod growers also will supply sprigs and plugs. Using certified seed or planting material ensures that it is true to type and relatively weed free.

Seeding and Mulching.

A well-prepared seedbed is essential for establishing turfgrasses. The seedbed should be tilled to a depth of 6 inches if possible, and fertilizer and other amendments worked into the soil prior to seeding. Prepare a smooth, firm seedbed; then divide the seed and sow in two directions, perpendicular to each other. If low rates of seed are being sown, mixing sawdust, organic fertilizer, or other suitable material with the seed aids in obtaining uniform coverage. Cover the seed by raking lightly and rolling. Avoid a smooth surface. A finished seedbed should have shallow uniform depressions (rows) about 1/2 inch deep and 1 to 2 inches apart such as are made by a corrugated roller.

Mulch the area with straw or other suitable material so that approximately 50 to 75 percent of the soil surface is covered. This is normally accomplished by spreading 1 1/2 to 2 bales of straw per 1,000 square feet. A light mulch does not need to be removed after establishment; however, a heavy mulch should be removed when the seedlings are about 2 inches tall. Avoid damaging the young seedlings during mulch removal. See *Table 1* for seeding rates.

Mixtures.

Fine fescues are often found in mixtures with Kentucky bluegrass. Fine fescues are best adapted to very shady conditions. A mixture of 50 percent bluegrass and 50 percent fine

Table 1. Recommended seeding rates (pounds of seed per 1,000 square feet) for major turfgrass species.

Species	High*	Medium**	Low***
Cool season			
Kentucky bluegrass	2-3	2-3	1-2
Perennial ryegrass	6-8	6-8	4-6
Tall fescue	8-10	8-10	8-10
Creeping bentgrass	1-2	1	Ø
Fine fescues	Ø	4-6	3-4
Warm season			
Buffalograss	Ø	1-3	1-2
Zoysiagrass	Ø	2-3	2-3

*Relatively high management inputs, such as golf course greens and fairways and sports turfs
**Golf course fairways, home turfs, or showcase grounds.
***Utility turfs, parks, or general grounds.
Ø Not recommended.

fescue by weight is recommended. Apply approximately 2 pounds/1,000 sq. ft. when seeding. **(Fine fescues are not the same as improved cultivars of tall fescue which have a finer leaf texture than older types of tall fescue such as Kentucky 31.)** Where quick establishment is desired, consider planting improved cultivars of perennial ryegrass in combination with Kentucky bluegrass. When perennial ryegrass is used with Kentucky bluegrass, do not exceed more than 1 pound ryegrass/1,000 sq. ft. or the bluegrass may be crowded out during establishment. Choose fine-textured perennial ryegrass cultivars with increased disease, heat, and cold tolerance, slower growth habits, and improved mowing qualities.

Mixtures to Avoid. Avoid using annual ryegrass, which is also known as Italian, domestic or common ryegrass. It establishes quickly, often at the expense of desirable grasses, and persists for only one season. Also avoid combining Kentucky bluegrass and older tall fescue varieties. The widely different growth habits and general appearance between these two turf species would provide for a very conflicting blend.

Sodding. Soil preparation should be similar to that described for seeding, but take care not to disturb the prepared soil by leaving deep footprints or wheel tracks. These depressions restrict root development and give an uneven appearance to the installed sod. During hot summer days, the soil should be dampened just prior to laying the sod. This avoids placing the turf roots in contact with excessively dry and hot soil.

Premium quality sod is easier to transport and install than inferior grades. Such sod is light, does not tear apart easily, and quickly generates a root system into the prepared soil. Before ordering or obtaining sod, be sure you are prepared to install it. Sod is perishable, and should not remain on the pallet or stack longer than 36 hours. The presence of mildew and distinct yellowing of the leaves is usually evidence of reduced turf vigor.

To reduce the need for short pieces when installing sod, it is generally best to establish a straight line lengthwise through the turf area. The sod can then be laid on either side of the line with the ends staggered as when laying bricks. A sharpened masonry trowel is very handy for cutting pieces, forcing the sod tight, and leveling small depressions. Immediately after the sod is laid, it should be rolled and kept very moist until it is well-rooted into the soil.

Plugging Warm Season Grasses. The best quality zoysiagrass must be vegetatively established using plugs. Buffalograss can be established by plugging or seeding. Again, the soil should be prepared as described for seeding. Plugs of zoysiagrass are commonly available, and are 1 to 2 inches in diameter with 1 to 2 inches of soil attached. The plugs should be fitted tightly into prepared holes and tamped firmly into place. Plugs are normally planted on 6- to 12-inch centers. Planting plugs on 6-inch centers requires 4,000 plugs per 1,000 square feet. On 12-inch centers, only 1,000 plugs are required per 1,000 square feet. Plugging buffalograss is comparable to plugging zoysiagrass except spacing up to 18-inch centers is acceptable.

Rake and/or Roll. Seed and vegetative materials must be in intimate contact with the soil for successful establishment. Raking is necessary for broadcast seeding to facilitate good soil to seed contact. Rolling will firm the soil and helps eliminate air pockets in sod installations.

Irrigation. Adequate moisture is critical to new turfgrass installations. Frequent light irrigation will be required until the new root system develops. Sod and plug installations must be thoroughly soaked so that the underlying soil is wet. Roots will not grow into dry soil.

Mowing. During initial establishment the turf should be mowed as frequently as possible. Mowing promotes lateral growth and spread and can significantly speedup establishment. The first mowing after establishment should occur as soon as the grass is high enough to mow at optimal height (*see Table 2*).

Renovation

Many turfgrass stands will decline over time, or it may be desirable to change species. The overseeding or conversion of a species is referred to as renovation. Many of the steps described in the previous section will be used for renovation with minor exceptions.

For conversion from one species to another it may be necessary to eradicate the existing species with a non-selective herbicide. This eradication is essential if the existing turf would be considered a weed in the new turf species. For within species cultivar conversion or overseeding bare spots, eradication is not necessary. Renovation with sod or sprigs will require a more aggressive site preparation like that required for new establishment.

Mowing

Mowing is the fundamental cultural practice on turfs. Improper mowing contributes to a thin, weak turf that is more susceptible to stress and injury.

Mowing Height

Cutting height will vary according to turfgrass species, intended use, intensity of culture, season, environment, and turf quality desired (*Table 2*).

Adjust the mowing height during the growing season to take advantage of variation in seasonal turfgrass growth habit and to modify the turf's growing environment. For example, mow Kentucky bluegrass at 2.0 inches in spring (mid-April to mid-June), 3.0 to 3.5 inches during summer (mid-June to late-August), and 2.0 inches in fall (early September until the last mowing).

In spring, maintain cool season species at the low end of their mowing range to take advantage of incoming radiation and soil warming for growth. Raise the cutting height during summer to increase the vegetation. This increase helps insulate the crown (growing point) from

Table 2. Recommended mowing heights for turfgrass grown in the Northern Great Plains.

Turfgrass	Seasonal mowing heights (inches)*		
	Spring	*Summer***	*Fall*
Cool season grasses			
Kentucky bluegrass	1.5 - 2.0	3.0 - 3.5	2.0
Perennial ryegrass	1.5 - 2.0	2.0 - 3.5	2.0
Tall fescue	2.0 - 3.0	3.0 - 3.5	2.0 - 3.0
Creeping red fescue	2.0	3.0	2.0
Chewings fescue	2.0	3.0	2.0
Hard fescue	2.0	3.0	2.0
Creeping bentgrass	3/32 - 1/2	3/16 - 5/8	3/32 - 1/2
Warm season grasses			
Zoysiagrass	1.0 - 2.0	1.0 - 2.0	1.5 - 2.0
Buffalograss	1.0 - 2.0	1.0 - 2.0	1.5 - 2.0
Blue grama	2.0	2.0	2.0

*Mowing heights within the ranges are based on climatic factors, intensity of culture, intended use, and quality of turf desired. Sports turf, such as golf courses or athletic fields, may be mowed shorter to facilitate playability.
**Use summer mowing heights when turfgrasses are grown in shaded conditions. Buffalograss and blue grama are not recommended for shaded areas.

high temperature stress and reduces weed competition. Gradually lower the mowing height in the fall. Lowering the mowing height promotes lateral turfgrass growth, stand thickening, and reduces overwintering debris.

Mowing Frequency

Mowing frequency is dictated by turfgrass growth rate. Do not remove more than 30 to 40 percent of the leaf blade with any mowing (*Figure 1*). For example, mow a Kentucky bluegrass turf maintained at 2.0 inches before it exceeds 3.0 to 3.5 inches. A mowing that removes an excessive amount of topgrowth is called scalping. Scalping reduces turf quality and restricts root growth. Severe defoliation that removes more than 50 percent of the topgrowth causes existing roots and rhizomes to stop growth. Tiller, rhizome, and root initiation cease and shoot regrowth will occur at the expense of the roots.

Lower the mowing height gradually if growth becomes excessive between mowings or when lowering the mowing height in the fall. Reduce the height in 0.5 to 1.0 inch increments, waiting two to three days between mowings, until turf is at the desired height.

Clipping Removal

Clippings don't need to be removed, except under specialized conditions, if proper mowing frequency is maintained. Clippings recycle nitrogen, phosphorus, and potassium to the turf. Clippings do not contribute to thatch build-up. Recycled clippings reduce the turfgrass nitrogen requirement for the growing season by as much as one-third. Remove clippings only if they accumulate during mowing. Grass clippings on the turf surface decompose slowly, may smother the grass, and enhance disease development. Use excess clippings for compost or air-dry clippings for use as a mulch in ornamental plantings.

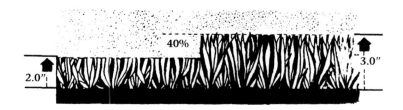

Figure 1. Do not remove more than 30-40 percent of the leaf with any mowing.

Mowing Equipment

Keep mower blades sharp and mowers properly adjusted and tuned. Improperly adjusted mowers give reduced mowing quality and are less fuel efficient. Mowers with dull blades mutilate the turfgrass leaf resulting in a browned appearance that reduces turfgrass quality, provides a favorable sitefor disease penetration, andresults in a weakened, more stress susceptible turf.

Fertilization

A fertilization program is important in a turf care program. You must consider several factors before the fertilizer program is developed:

1. Soil test
2. Soil type
3. Turfgrass species and cultivar
4. Intensity of culture
5. Irrigation practices
6. Clipping removal and return
7. Type and cost of fertilizer
8. Convenience of fertilizer application

Soil Tests

Turfgrasses depend on soils for their nutritional needs. It is important to test the soil every three to five years to determine available nutrients. More frequent testing is required when dealing with a problem soil, nutrient deficiency, or pH modification. Most soil tests analyze pH, potassium, and phosphorus levels. Turfgrass nitrogen requirements are usually based on turfgrass evaluations rather than soil test results.

Randomly collect 10 to 20 soil samples from the turf, using a clean, narrow garden tool or soil probe. Sample the upper 3 inches of soil. Discard the turf and thatch. Combine the samples in a plastic container, allow to air dry, and mix thoroughly. Send a pint of soil to a reputable soil testing lab, specifying whether the sample is from a new or established turf. Most Cooperative Extension offices can supply information on sampling procedures and a soil sample container to mail samples to the area University Soil Testing Laboratory.

Turfgrasses require 16 essential nutrients for their growth and development:

Macronutrients

Carbon	Calcium
Hydrogen	Magnesium
Oxygen	Sulfur
Nitrogen	Potassium
Phosphorus	

Micronutrients

Iron	Molybdenum
Manganese	Boron
Zinc	Chlorine
Copper	

The turfgrass plant requires these elements in varying amounts, and will suffer if any of these elements is not present in adequate amounts.

Carbon, hydrogen, and oxygen are supplied to the plant from the atmosphere and water. The remaining essential nutrients must be supplied by the soil. When adequate levels are not found in the soil, the essential elements must be supplied from fertilizers.

The fertilizer label contains information concerning what the product contains. The label indicates the percentage of nitrogen (N), available phosphate (P_2O_5), and water soluble potash (K_2O) (*Figure 2*).

Turfgrass fertilizers vary based on the analysis. Most turfgrass specialists recommend fertilizers with ratios (i.e. $N:P_2O_5:K_2O$) of 4:1:2, 3:1:2, or similar ones for maintaining established turfs. Higher ratios of phosphate and potash are recommended on newly seeded or sodded turfs.

In most cases, slow-release nitrogen fertilizer sources or a combination of slow and fast-release, are preferred over fast-release fertilizers alone (*Table 3*). If a fast-release nitrogen source must be used, it is best to use light, frequent applications rather than heavy, infrequent ones. Fertilizer programs emphasizing slow-release sources result in uniform turfgrass shoot and root growth over a longer time than those using fast-release sources.

Nitrogen

Turfgrasses respond most readily to nitrogen if other nutrients are present in adequate amounts. Nitrogen influences shoot and root growth, color, density, recuperative rate, and stress hardiness, such as heat, cold, and drought hardiness. It is

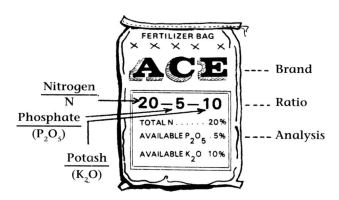

Figure 2. Parts of the fertilizer label.

11

Table 3. Nitrogen carrier examples for turfgrass fertilization.

Carrier[a]	N	P_2O_5	K_2O	Amount (lb) needed to apply 1 lb N per 1000 sq. ft.
Fast Release	- - - - - % - - - - -			
Ammonium nitrate	33.0	—	—	3.0
Ammonium sulfate	20.5	—	—	4.9
Urea	45.0	—	—	2.2
Slow Release				
Activated sewage sludge (eg. Milorganite)	4-7	4-6	0.4-0.7	16.7
Sulfur-Coated Urea	36.0	—	—	2.7
IBDU	31.0	—	—	3.2
Urea formaldehyde	38.0	—	—	2.6

[a]This list is not all-inclusive.

important to maintain a controlled level of nitrogen nutrition and not fertilize above recommended levels (*Table 4*). Too much nitrogen results in succulent growth susceptible to heat and drought stress injury, and prone to insect and disease problems.

Several types of nitrogen carriers are available. Fast-release sources make nitrogen available to the plant quickly, resulting in a rapid, short-lived response. They have a high potential for burning the grass and promoting succulent growth. As a result they should not be applied at rates higher than one pound of actual nitrogen per 1000 square feet. Slow-release sources make nitrogen

available to the turfgrass plant over a longer time period. Turfgrass response to slow-release nitrogen sources is not as rapid and potential for foliar burn is lower than for rapid-release sources. For best results use a combination of fast- and slow-release nitrogen.

Potassium and Phosphorus

Use soil test results to determine the need for additional phosphorus and potassium. Higher rates of phosphorus are recommended on newly seeded areas. Phosphorus affects establishment and root development, and potassium influences turfgrass wear, heat, cold, and drought tolerance.

Table 4. Annual nitrogen requirements for turfgrass species used in the Northern Great Plains.

Turfgrass species	Amount of nitrogen required each growing season (lb/1000 ft^2)[a]
Improved Kentucky bluegrass (i.e. Baron, Glade, Midnight, etc.)	3 to 6
Common Kentucky bluegrass (i.e. Park, Newport, Delta, Cougar, Kenblue, etc.)	2 to 4
Perennial ryegrass	3 to 6
Tall fescue	1 to 4
Fine-leaf fescues (i.e. Creeping red, Chewings, Hard, and Sheep fescue)	1 to 4
Creeping bentgrass	3 to 6
Zoysiagrass	1 to 3
Buffalograss	0 to 2
Blue grama	0 to 2

[a]Nitrogen recommendations are based on a six-month growing season. A range for nitrogen is given because of variations in soil, climate, cultural practices, intensity of management, and clipping return or removal.

Fertilizer Timing

Timing of fertilizer applications depends upon turfgrass species, turf quality desired, cultural intensity, turfgrass use, and soil nutrient retention.

All turfs need to be fertilized at least once a year. Warm season turfgrasses require a different fertilization schedule than cool season turfgrasses. Fertilize cool season turfgrasses in late fall (mid October to mid November). Warm season turfgrasses should be fertilized before Aug. 15. Applications after this date encourage weed competition and winter injury.

High maintenance turfs require nutrients throughout the growing season (*Table 5*).

A general fertilization schedule for a high maintenance, cool season turf would include four applications of fertilizer per growing season.

Avoid heavy fertilizer applications in early spring (March and early April). Early spring applications increase disease susceptibility, high temperature stress, and drought injury. Turfs that are frequently watered, have clippings removed, or grow on coarse, sandy soils require more fertilizer more frequently than turfs which are watered less frequently and have their clippings returned.

Do not fertilize during high temperature stress conditions on cool season turfgrasses. Light applications of 0.5 pound of nitrogen per 1,000

Table 5. A typical schedule for fertilizing Kentucky bluegrass at a medium to high maintenance level.

Application	Timing	Nitrogen/ 1000 sq. ft.
1	April 20 to May 10	0.5 to 1 pound
2	June 5 to June 15	0.75 to 1 pound
3	September 1 to September 15	0.75 to 1 pound
4	October 15 to November 15	1 to 1.5 pounds

square feet or less can enhance turfgrass color and recovery from insect or disease damage.

Iron Deficiency

In the Northern Great Plains many soils can be alkaline or have a high pH. Turf growing on high pH soils may exhibit a uniform yellow appearance, even when adequately supplied with nitrogen. This appearance is often the result of an iron deficiency. Iron deficiency occurs in high pH soils because the iron in the soil is unavailable for grass uptake. Confirmation of iron deficiency can be made by closely examining a turfgrass leaf (*see page 173 for photo*). If the yellowing is between the leaf veins (i.e. interveinal) this may indicate an iron deficiency. Adding sulfur may lower the pH sufficiently to release soil iron but will require repeat applications. Some turfgrass fertilizers,

especially in areas where iron deficiency is common, may also contain iron in forms that the turfgrass plant can utilize. Foliar application of iron is, however, the most effective means of correcting an iron deficient turf.

Late Season Fertilization

Nitrogen recommendations have changed for cool season grasses, placing emphasis on late season rather than spring fertilizer applications. As temperatures cool, rainfall increases, and turfgrasses come out of summer dormancy, fertilizer plays an important role in root growth and carbohydrate storage within the plant. Nitrogen applied in late fall stimulates some topgrowth, but not to the extent that occurs in spring.

As top growth slows, carbo-hydrates produced are stored or used in the growth of

14

underground structures such as roots and rhizomes. The greatest rhizome growth occurs in the fall. This growth increases the density of a Kentucky bluegrass turf. Late season fertilizer programs do not eliminate the need for spring fertilization but allow the turfgrass manager to use lighter rates that give uniform shoot and root growth. The late season application improves fall and winter color retention, stress tolerance, root growth, and spring green-up.

Apply fertilizer about the time of the last mowing of the season. This usually takes place in late October or early November. Apply fertilizer at a rate of 1 to 1.5 pounds of nitrogen per 1,000 square feet. Do not apply fertilizer after the turf has become brown or the soil is frozen. Under these conditions significant amounts of nutrients can be lost due to surface runoff, leaching, or both.

Fertilize to meet the nutritional needs of the turf. An inadequately fertilized turf is more susceptible to weeds, diseases, and insects. Too much fertilizer increases susceptibility to disease and environmental stress. Follow label directions carefully for rate, timing, application method, and recommended use.

Irrigation

by Don Steinegger, Extension Ornamental Specialist

Irrigation is necessary in the Northern Great Plains to maintain a healthy, vigorous turf. The turf plant is 75-80 percent water by weight. A small reduction in water content can be lethal to the plant. The need for supplemental irrigation varies among turfgrass species. If the drought period is extended, even the most drought tolerant grasses will need supplemental watering.

Frequency

Base watering frequency on the turfgrass plant's need. Look for signs of wilting before applying water and avoid regularly scheduled watering with automatic systems. A dark, blue-green color and footprints which remain after walking on the turf are signs that it needs water. When these conditions occur, irrigate the turf as thoroughly as pos–sible without causing runoff or puddling. Repeat this process several times until the soil is well-moistened. Amount and frequency of watering depends on: 1) turfgrass species and cultivar, 2) soil texture and structure, 3) ground slope, 4) exposure, 5) climate, 6) intensity of culture and use, and 7) length of growing season.

Irrigation Timing

Early morning (4 a.m. to 8 a.m.) is the best time to water. The least demand for water is placed on municipal systems at this time, wind and evaporative losses are low, application efficiency is high, and distribution is best. Midday watering is not hazardous to the turf but is inefficient and should be avoided. Evaporative losses are greatest at midday and wind makes it difficult to apply water uniformly.

A form of midday watering, called syringing, is beneficial for turfs to minimize high temperature stress. This light application of water evaporates rapidly from leaf blade surfaces. The evaporation process cools the turf and reduces heat stress. Syringing is also beneficial for turfs with active Summer Patch disease.

Avoid watering in the early evening or at night because it can increase disease problems. Evaporative water loss is low and relative humidity is high at night. Night watering favors dew formation and its duration. Water remains on the leaf surface and enhances turfgrass disease growth and development. Night watering may be necessary in some cases, but it should be used only when early morning watering cannot be practiced.

How to Water

Water turfs thoroughly, infrequently, and uniformly to develop a deep, extensive root system. Infrequent (i.e. five to seven days), but thorough watering encourages the plant to develop a deep root system. Frequent (i.e. daily), light watering results in a shallow root system. Plants with shallow root systems are prone to heat and drought stress and damage from disease and insects.

To thoroughly wet a clay soil, it may require several light water applications. After the soil is moist allow five to seven days before rewetting.

Beauty and utility have traditionally been the purposes of home and commercial landscapes. Because water — in both quality and quantity — is becoming a limited resource, conservation has become a third goal. One can achieve all three by using careful, comprehensive planning.

You can reduce water consumption by 40 to 80 percent by following an appropriate sequence in designing and managing a site: 1) develop a well planned design, 2) use adapted, drought-tolerant plants, 3) irrigate properly, 4) improve the soil, 5) mulch, and 6) use appropriate, timely maintenance.

A properly designed and functioning irrigation system saves water, improves plant appearance, and reduces non-point source pollution. An irrigation system must apply water uniformly, at a rate that the soil can absorb, and in the proper amount to meet the water needs of the landscape plants. Runoff can result when an improperly functioning system applies water faster than the soil can absorb the water. This runoff can carry applied fertilizer, such as nitrogen, and some pesticides into the streets and eventually into storm drains. Excess irrigation water entering the soil can result in nitrogen and pesticides moving below the root zone and eventually reaching the groundwater. Uniform water application helps to assure no portion of the landscape is over or under watered.

Does the irrigation system apply water uniformly? Uniformity means that every plant or soil surface should receive the same amount of water. For example, one area should not receive 1/2 inch of water while another area receives 1 1/2 inches. Non-uniform applications result in having to over-water one area to assure another won't dry out.

Uniformity is achieved through proper spacing and placement of sprinkler heads. Space heads closer together than design specifications require. This slight increase of installation cost is easily justified by reduced water use and enhanced plant quality.

Another factor to adjust in an irrigation system is water pressure. Proper pressure helps minimize the effect of wind. Excessive water pressure creates small particles of water which the wind easily moves away from the planned application pattern. Distorted patterns mean some landscape area will require addi-tional watering even after sufficient water has gone through the system.

One can reduce the effect of wind by watering just after sunrise when wind is minimal. However, a system should be designed for the highest wind speeds expected during the growing season.

Efficient irrigation also considers ways to reduce runoff. It is important to understand the soil character-istics of a site. "Heavy soils," such as clay, have infiltration rates often less than 1/2 inch per hour. Adjust the system accordingly: usually don't apply more than 1/2 inch per hour. If a landscape needs more water, add another 1/2 inch the next day.

A final factor in efficient irrigation is the one that is

most often forgotten: a landscape may have changed since installation. Increased size of plant material may now block or distort the spray pattern. Modify either the plants or the irrigation system.

Do the following tests to determine the proper application rate and uniformity of your system.

Test 1

Select flat-bottomed, straight-sided containers, such as coffee or tuna cans. Space the cans uniformly 10 to 15 feet apart (do not exceed 15 feet apart). Irrigate, i.e., run a system for at least 15 minutes and then measure the depth of the water in each can. Use a ruler or mark the inside of the cans in 1/2 inch increments.

Table 6 contains the water depth values obtained when six cans were placed on a turf and the irrigation system was run for 15 minutes. With the information from *Table 6*, you can determine how long a system needs to run to apply an average of 1 inch to the turf area.

Use the information in *Table 7* to determine the number of minutes to run an irrigation system to apply the proper amount of water.

For example, assume an irrigation system applies an average of 3/8 inch in 15 minutes. Go to the 3/8 inch value to determine the time for a system to apply one inch of water. Below the 3/8 inch value is the number 40. This is the number of minutes your system needs to apply 1 inch of water.

Test 2

The next information needed is the infiltration rate for the soil in a given landscape. Use the same kind of can as for the previous test, but cut out the bottom. Mark the inside of the can in 1-inch increments. Insert one end of the can into the soil. Be sure it goes through both turf and thatch. Check that water does not seep laterally from the

Table 6. Water depths obtained from the Catch-Can Test run for 15 minutes to determine the system's watering rate.

	Can Number						Water Total (inches)
1	2	3	4	5	6		
3/8"	7/16"	5/16"	5/16	3/8"	7/16"		36/16"

Average depth (inches): Total divided by 6 cans equals 6/16" or 3/8"

Average application is 3/8" in 15 minutes.

Table 7. Operation time needed for a system to apply an average of 1 inch of water, after you have measured the water delivered in 15 minutes.

	Average Depth of Water in Cans (Inches)										
	1/8	3/16	1/4	5/16	3/8	7/16	1/2	9/16	5/8	11/16	3/4
Time (min)	120	80	60	48	40	34	30	27	24	22	20

can. Fill the can with water and allow time for all of it to drain into the soil. Then add water to the two-inch mark on the can. Now measure the time for this water to sink into the soil. Divide this elapsed time by 2. The number you get will be the infiltration rate for a given turf site, i.e., the rate for 1 inch of water to enter your soil. Adjust the irrigation system to apply water at, or below, this rate.

To increase even further the efficient use of water, group together plants with similar water, soil, light, and nutrient requirements. By grouping together plants with similar needs, one can install a zone water irrigation system. That is, one valve and one clock station on the controller will serve all the plants within each zone.

With zone watering you won't overwater one plant or site while underwatering another plant or site. For example, Buffalograss requires less frequent irrigation than Kentucky bluegrass. Also, a windy, sunny site generally requires more water than a

shady, protected area. Zone watering allows you to divide your landscape into specific water needs areas.

Initially the cost is greater for a water-conserving system; however, the long-term benefits will include saving water, reducing pollution, and providing for healthier, more attractive plants.

Irrigation System Components and Trouble Shooting

It is a common misconception that an irrigation system will perform indefinitely without service or adjustments. Problems will develop, but they are correctable. Some will be beyond the do-it-yourselfer's skills and will require those of an irrigation specialist. This section walks you through an evaluation of an irrigation system, including the control system, zoning of stations, and physical condition of the system components. It covers the main categories a specialist uses to evaluate an irrigation system. Working through the

19

procedures described in this section will identify conditions that lead to wasting water. While certain steps only apply to installed systems, others are relevant to a hose and hose-end sprinkler system.

Control System

Identify the controller or time clocks. These determine when and how long the sys– tem or each station runs. Also evaluate the condition of con– trol system components. Look for bad connections, frayed wires, and unreadable indica- tors. If the system includes an electro-mechanical clock, does it keep accurate time and operate the system as programmed? If not, you may want to replace it with an electronic model that is more accurate. Be sure your control- ler is sufficiently flexible to 1) allow easy change in watering schedules, 2) irrigate turf and shrubs separately (zone watering), and 3) operate in short irrigation cycles to prevent runoff. Make a list of all of the stations and describe the locations to which each applies irrigation water. Place it in the controller for future reference.

Valve Condition

A valve is a device that controls the flow of water through a pipe. A typical irrigation system valve will be either fully closed or open. To check for leaks, turn off all water and read the meter. After 12 hours (do it overnight when no water is being used for any purpose), read it again. If the meter hand has moved, check for leaks. Leaks often occur at valves. Make sure that valves open when the controller calls for water- ing of the zone controlled by each valve. If the controller has a battery back-up, check the charge on the battery.

Wiring Condition

Inspect visible wiring for breaks, poor connections, or broken insulation. Malfunc- tioning valves can result from wiring problems. You can verify by checking wire voltages. If you find problems, hire a qualified professional to make repairs.

Back Flow Prevention

City codes require that a backflow prevention device be installed on irrigation systems. This device prevents any flow from the irrigation system back into the water system within a home. This assures that your drinking water will not be contami- nated. Install a backflow prevention device even when not required. Check the local building code inspection for regulations in your area. Some backflow prevention devices may have a way to check to be sure the device is functioning properly.

Soil Moisture Sensors

These can be wired into the controller to start the irrigation system when a given soil moisture level is reached. This helps to assure that the plant needs are met and that unneeded irrigation is not applied. Placement of the sensors is critical. Place them in the plants' root zone within the area covered by the irrigation system. Check to make sure the sensor is operating properly. Sensors differ in the way they work, so check manufacturer's directions for proper installation and operation. Sensors also can be used with hose and hose-end sprinkler systems.

Rainfall Sensor

These sensors can be integrated into the controller to override programmed irrigations after a given sized rainfall. This is an important water saving device. Observe the system after receiving rain to be sure the sensor is functioning properly.

Pressure Regulator

An irrigation system may have a pressure reducing valve. This is true for both sprinkler and drip irrigation systems. Excessive pressure results in fogging and misting and even the physical bursting of system components. Misting creates very fine droplets and distorts spray patterns, causing non-uniform water distribution and water waste. Insufficient pressure, however, causes inadequate break-up of sprinkler spray patterns and uneven discharge rates from sprinklers or emitters. Green "doughnuts" around sprinklers are a sign of low pressure.

Install at least two pressure regulators if the system uses a sprinkler for turf and drip for shrubs and flower borders. Two regulators may be required if a combination of impact or other rotating spray type sprinklers are used.

Pressure regulator function can be evaluated by checking the pressure at various locations within the system. Pressure will not be equal at all points because of friction loss as water flows through the pipe system and elevation changes.

Landscape Zones

Each zone (different areas of irrigation control) of the irrigation system needs to be evaluated. See the "checklist" for the factors to evaluate.

Avoid mixing plant types that have vastly different water requirements in the same watering zone. For example, Kentucky bluegrass and yews should not be in the same zone. Yews will not survive the amount of water required for Kentucky bluegrass. Also, avoid a single station that waters both sunny and shady areas.

Frequently, the irrigation system was installed before materials were planted in the landscape. When the landscape matures, trees interfere with spray patterns. Contact an irrigation designer/installer to change or reset the heads to irrigate the area effectively or do it yourself.

Physical Problems

The three common physical problems in an irrigation system are broken components such as risers, improperly designed or spaced heads, and dissimilar heads or nozzles.

Check rotation and direction of spray. Adjust the radius and arc to avoid spraying sidewalks and buildings. Physical problems with the system result in lack of application uniformity. As a consequence, wet and dry spots develop. Also, as the system ages and the landscape matures, sprinkler heads sink, or heads are pushed off vertical, stop turning, or become clogged. All of these physical problems affect the spray pattern.

Clean the sprinkler's trash filter screen if it has one. Check the wiper seal at the base of the sprinkler heads. Water will squirt out of the base if it is worn. Make corrections to assure that proper operation and water distribution occurs.

While a hose and hose-end sprinkler system lacks many of these components, the checklist is still valuable in evaluating the proper use of this system and the effectiveness of the hose end sprinkler.

Drains — Winterizing the Irrigation System

An irrigation system can be drained by either blowing the water out of the irrigation lines or draining the pipe lines with an automatic or a manual drain valve located at the low point of the system. Check with an authorized turf irrigation specialist to see that these drain valves are functioning properly and not leaking.

On home lawn systems with back flow preventers use the procedures outlined in *Figure 3* for proper drainage and start-up procedures.

Soil Cultivation

Many soils have high clay and silt content. These soils are prone to compaction when exposed to traffic, irrigation, and rainfall. Soil

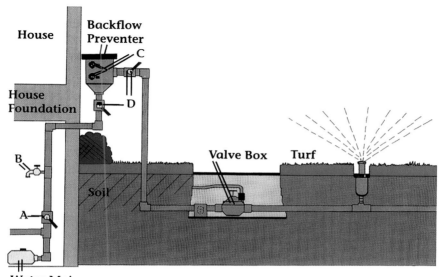

Figure 3. Proper drainage and start-up procedures for home lawn irrigation systems.

Fall Sprinkler Drainage Procedure:

1. Close Valve "A".
2. Open Valve "B" (use bucket to collect drainage).
3. Open Valves "C" (often requires flat head screw-driver).
4. Do not adjust Valves "D".
5. Start controller and let system run through a complete watering cycle. No heads will come up when you do this.
6. Turn controller to "Off" at the completion of the watering cycle.

Spring Sprinkler Start-Up Procedure:

1. Close Valve "B".
2. Close Valves "C" (often requires flat head screw-driver).
3. Do not adjust Valves "D". They should remain fully open.
4. Open Valve "A".
5. Be sure to put a fresh battery in your controller (if it requires one). If your controller was plugged in over the winter, your fall watering schedule should remain intact. If you have unplugged your controller over the winter, you must reprogram it.

compaction reduces turfgrass quality, growth, and vigor by decreasing soil aeration, water infiltration, and root growth. Soil cultivation (coring, slicing, and spiking) relieves compaction and enhances turfgrass growth (*Figure 4*).

Aerify sites prone to compaction at least once and preferably twice each year. Aerify when the turfgrass is actively growing to enhance recovery and maximize root growth responses. Control traffic on areas prone to compaction to minimize problems. Turfs established on poor soils or highly disturbed soils associated with new building sites require more frequent aerification. These sites should be aerified twice each year.

Thatch

Thatch is located between the green vegetation and the soil surface. It consists of a layer of dead and decaying turfgrass tissues derived from leaves, shoots, and roots.

Thatch accumulates when the rate of turfgrass organic matter production exceeds its rate of decomposition. Small amounts (less than 1/2 inch) can be beneficial. Some thatch increases the turf's resiliency, improves wear

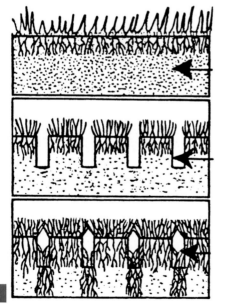

Compaction is greatest in the first inch or two of soil.

Coring device removes soil cores.

Rooting depth is improved.

Figure 4. Soil cultivation with a coring device enhances water, air, and nutrient penetration, as well as increases root depth.

Thatch is a layer of dead and decaying tissue located between the green vegetation and the soil.

tolerance, and insulates against soil temperature changes. Thatch accumulations more than 1/2 inch reduce heat, cold, and drought hardiness and increase localized dry spots, scalping, disease, and insect problems. As thatch accumulates, there is a tendency for root and rhizome growth to occur in the thatch layer rather than in the soil (*Figure 5*). This situation is particularly troublesome since thatch build-up is accelerated by root and rhizome tissue debris. Without proper thatch management, the turf will become poorly rooted and prone to stress injury.

Figure 5. As thatch accumulates, turfgrass roots grow in the thatch rather than in the soil, resulting in a weakened turf prone to stress injury.

To evaluate thatch accumulation, cut a pie-shaped wedge of grass and soil and measure the organic matter between the green vegetation and the soil.

To determine thatch accumulation, cut a pie-shaped wedge of grass and soil, remove it, and measure the organic matter that has accumulated. Measure the accumulation from several areas in the turf, since thatch is not uniformly distributed. If the layer exceeds 1/2 inch, the thatch accumulation needs to be reduced.

Thatch can be removed by hand raking or by using a power rake. Hand raking is laborious and is only practical for small areas. Power rakes use rigid wire tines or steel blades to lift thatch debris and a small amount of soil to the turf surface. The soil should be moist for best results. Power raking during excessive soil moisture conditions tears and pulls the turf from the soil instead of slicing and lifting the thatch debris as desired. Remove thatch during periods of active turfgrass growth. Thatch removal from cool season turfgrasses, like Kentucky bluegrass, is best done in the early spring and in the fall after Labor Day. Remove the thatch when at least 30 days of favorable growing conditions will occur after dethatching. Thatch removal in the spring requires an application of preemergent herbicide to prevent establishment of annual weeds.

Core cultivation (aerification) can be used to minimize thatch accumulation, to modify its physical characteristics, and to remove limited amounts of thatch. Core cultivation is not as effective as power raking in removing thatch debris but is more effective in reducing thatch accumulation rate. A combination of soil cultivation and aeration is a preferred program to modify and reduce thatch build-up.

If mechanical thatch removal is necessary, do it when the turf is actively growing to aid in recovery. Fall is the preferred time because weed competition is minimal. Spring is an acceptable time, but apply a preemergent herbicide after dethatching to prevent establishment of annual weeds. Power rake lightly, removing no more than 1/2 inch of thatch at a time. If thatch is

excessive, it may require several spring and fall treatments. In some cases it may be necessary to completely renovate or reestablish the turf.

Pesticides

Pesticides are part of integrated pest management (IPM) programs, but they are only a tool to be used as needed in an overall plant management approach. Pesticides for turfs include: fungicides for diseases, insecticides for insects, and herbicides for weed control. These materials should be used as directed by label information and applied only as needed.

Use well-adapted turfgrass species and cultivars to reduce disease and insect problems. Proper mowing, fertilizing, and watering reduce weed problems. These steps reduce the need for pesticides to produce a quality turf. Considerable information is available from Cooperative Extension that can help turf managers make the right decisions on grass selection and management. These decisions will reduce the need for pesticides to produce a quality turf.

A Common Sense Approach

The integrated pest management (IPM) approach to turf care is a common sense approach. It might best be described as "integrated turfgrass management" since IPM develops turfs that have greater potential to resist pest problems.

A vigorous, well maintained turf has the potential to withstand higher insect, disease, and weed populations without causing detrimental effects on the turf. Proper cultural practices promote turf growth to aid in resisting these infestations. Pesticides are a tool that can be used in IPM programs. Use them only as needed. IPM approaches reduce the need for pesticides when growing a quality turfgrass stand.

CULTURAL PRACTICES

Preferred mowing height in inches	Irrigation require-ment	Disease problems	Insect problems	COMMENTS
1.5 to 2.5	yes	some	some	Use a blend of three or more improved cultivars.
1.75 to 3.5	seldom	seldom	seldom	Good low maintenance turfgrass. Direct low temperature kill is a problem.
1.5 to 2.5	yes	some	some	Some improved cultivars are available with improved mowing quality and improved high and low temperature tolerance.
1.0 to 2.5	yes	some	seldom	Mixes well with Kentucky bluegrass, should be included in mixes where shade is a problem.
1.0 to 2.5	yes	some	seldom	Rapid establishment on sandy areas, bunch-type grass, shade tolerant.
1.25 to 2.5	some	some	seldom	Somewhat better disease resistance than creeping red fescue. Mixes well with Kentucky bluegrass.
.1 to .5	yes	yes	yes	Use in Northern Great Plains limited to golf course greens and fairways.
0.5 to 1.0	seldom	seldom	seldom	Slow to establish but forms a dense, weed resistant turf.
0.5 to 3.0	no	seldom	seldom	Good low maintenance turfgrass, somewhat susceptible to phenoxy herbicide injury.
1.5 to 3.0	no	seldom	seldom	Mixes well with buffalo-grass. Not recommended in monostands.

Insects and Related Pests of Turfgrass

Frederick P. Baxendale
Extension Entomologist

- Understanding Integrated Pest Management (IPM)
- Cultural control practices
- Biological control
- Insecticides
- White grubs
- Billbugs
- Sod webworms
- Cutworms and armyworms
- Chinch bugs
- Greenbugs
- Leafhoppers
- Spider mites
- Ants

nsect management is important in the overall care of turfgrass. Today's turf manager must not only be able to accurately diagnose insect problems as they occur, but also anticipate future problems. This chapter presents an integrated approach to managing insects and related pests of turfgrass.

The IPM Philosophy

Recent concerns over environmental safety, the loss of long-term residual insecticides, and a growing awareness of the problems associated with the overuse of pesticides have reemphasized the importance of developing efficient and environmentally sound methods for managing turfgrass pests. Integrated pest management (IPM) is a system or strategy which uses all suitable methods and techniques in a compatible manner to maintain pest densities below levels causing unacceptable injury.

Inherent in the IPM philosophy is the recognition that for most pests, population levels exist that can be tolerated without significant plant injury. The turfgrass manager does not attempt to eradicate

a pest because moderate pest levels help maintain natural enemies, and chemical overuse can lead to pesticide resistance. The overall objective of IPM is to optimize rather than maximize pest control.

An important aspect of IPM involves planning to avoid or minimize future pest problems. Decisions made during the establishment and maintenance of a turf area can significantly influence pest development. Among these key decisions are selection of turfgrass species and cultivar, weed and disease control strategies, irrigation, fertilization, thatch management, and other cultural practices which affect the health and vigor of the turfgrass. As a general rule, stressed or poorly maintained turf will exhibit pest damage sooner than healthy turf, and will be slower to recover after insect or mite injury.

Despite appropriate measures to avoid or reduce insect problems, pest populations may increase under certain conditions. When using IPM, control measures including conventional pesticides are employed only when pest numbers reach or threaten to reach predetermined levels or "treatment thresholds."

These thresholds are flexible guidelines that are usually defined as the level of insect

Graphics and slides for this chapter were prepared by Jim Kalisch, Extension Technologist, Entomology, unless otherwise credited.

abundance or damage that can be tolerated before taking action. They are typically based on several variables including pest species, abundance, and life stage; variety, vigor, and value of the turfgrass; relative effectiveness and cost of control measures; and time of year. Treatment thresholds are not hard rules that apply to every situation, but when used conscientiously, they should help turfgrass managers make effective pest management decisions.

Implementing an IPM Program for Turfgrass

Establishing a pest management program requires a sound understanding of the growth habits and cultural requirements of the turfgrass; knowledge of the biology, behavior, life history, and type of damage caused by potential pests; and information regarding the time of year, growth stage of the turfgrass, and environmental conditions under which pest damage is most likely to occur. Accurate pest identification is also important. In addition, turfgrass managers must integrate insect control with disease, weed, and cultural management strategies.

Categories of Turf-Damaging Insects

Turf insects can be categorized into two groups based on their feeding location: 1) soil-active insects that damage turf by feeding below the soil surface on the plant's underground stems and root system, and 2) surface-active insects that feed on above ground portions of plants.

In general, soil-active insects are more damaging to turf than surface feeders because injury occurs below the growing point, making it more difficult for the plant to outgrow the injury. Also, soil-active insects are more difficult to detect and are protected from most natural enemies and adverse environmental conditions. Examples of soil-active insects include white grubs, billbug larvae, and some soil cutworms.

By contrast, surface-feeders damage plants above the growing point and are generally less injurious to the plant. Insects such as sod webworms, most cutworms, and armyworms defoliate the turf by feeding on grass blades, while other pests including greenbugs, chinch bugs, and spider mites feed by sucking juices from leaves and stems. In general, surface-active pests are more susceptible to natural enemies and are much easier to detect.

Pest Identification

All turfgrasses are inhabited by a diverse array of organisms including insects, spiders, mites, nematodes, and many other small animals. Most of these cause little or no damage and are generally considered non-pests. Others serve important beneficial roles in the breakdown of thatch, aerification of the soil or as natural enemies of insect and mite pests. Only a few of the species present are actually plant-feeding pests. Because of the many similarities between pests and non-pests, it is essential that the turf manager be able to distinguish incidental and beneficial species from target pests.

Early Detection

Successful management of most turf insects depends on detecting pests before they reach damaging levels. This can be accomplished best through frequent turf inspections to detect early signs of insects and their damage.

Among the more common symptoms of insect-damaged turf are a general thinning of the grass, spongy areas, irregular brown patches and/ or plants which easily break away at soil level. Substantiating the insect-origin of the problem may be difficult, however, because many of these symptoms could also have been caused by non-insect factors such as heat or drought stress, nutritional deficiencies, turf diseases, soil compaction, chemical burns from gasoline, fertilizers, herbicides or insecticides, scalping during mowing operations, or even animal excrement. If the problem is insect-related, a close examination should reveal either the presence of the pest or indirect evidence of an insect infestation.

Bird and animal feeding often indicates a potential insect problem. Flocks of foraging birds, particularly starlings and robins, and/or digging and tunnelling by skunks, raccoons, moles, or other animals are common, early indicators of insect infestations. Other signs of an existing infestation or potential problems include large numbers of masked chafer beetles, armyworm or cutworm moths around lights, billbug adults on sidewalks and driveways, or sod webworm moths flying over lawns in the process of depositing their eggs.

Confirmation of the insect origin of the problem requires close examination of the injured area. Look for signs of skeletonized leaves, clipped grass blades, fecal pellets, sawdust-like debris, stem tunneling, silken tubes or webbing. Refer to individual sections in this chapter for a description of the symptoms of damage caused by specific insects. If no insects or evidence of feeding are found, the condition is probably due to some other cause, and an insecticide would not be of value.

Insect Monitoring Techniques

All turf areas should be regularly inspected for pest problems throughout the growing season. Monitoring allows the turfgrass manager to confirm the presence or absence of an insect or mite pest, determine the pest species present, assess the need for taking corrective measures, evaluate the efficacy of insecticide treatments, and develop site history information.

Insect monitoring techniques include observation, soil sampling, use of irritants (e. g., detergents, Detect-Aid), pitfall traps, flotation devices, and sweep nets. Light and pheromone traps also can be used to monitor the seasonal occurrence of insects as an indicator of when to start sampling for specific pests. Since most insect and mite pests of turf do not distribute themselves evenly throughout the turf, it is essential that the turfgrass area be sampled in a consistent, uniform pattern. Enough samples should be taken to assure a reasonably accurate estimate of pest numbers in the sampled area. If turf damage is evident but no pests are detected, examine the turf for other causes of injury such as disease, excessive thatch, improper mowing, heat or moisture stress. Watch for beneficial natural enemies, such as lady beetles, big-eyed bugs, lacewings, ground beetles, spiders, and parasitic wasps that may be reducing pest populations.

Surface-active insects often can be detected by applying 1/4 cup of lemon-scented household detergent or one tablespoon of 1 percent pyre–thrins in 2 gallons of water poured over 1 square yard of turf. These preparations irritate webworms, cutworms, billbug adults, and other surface feeding pests, causing them to move to the surface in five to ten minutes, where they can be counted.

For soil-active insects such as white grubs and billbug lar-vae, verify activity by cutting 1/4 square foot (6" X 6") sections of turf on three sides, peeling back the sod and examining the upper 2 inches of root zone for pests. Turfgrass managers with access to a golf course cup cutter can sample for soil-inhabiting insects by taking 4-inch (0.1 square foot) diameter turf-soil cores.

Record-keeping

Accurate record-keeping is essential for the success of a turfgrass pest management program. Records should be as complete as possible and include the kinds and numbers of pests present, when and where they were found, and exact locations and extent of any turf damage or abnormalities observed. Information on the turf species and cultivar development, turf health, and current environmental conditions is also valuable. When recording scouting or other management information be as quantitative as possible. Record the number of insects per unit area and assign damage ratings to injured turf (e.g. 1 = severe damage, 3 = moderate damage, 5 = no observable damage). Avoid vague designations such as high or low, or heavy or light. At the end of the season, review this information and plan to improve your pest management program next year. You may have detected certain patterns, such as a greater number of pests or more damage in some areas or associated with certain cultivars which will help you focus scouting and management activities.

Effective record-keeping also allows you to know when to expect certain pest problems and plan ahead to deal with them. Also, information from regular inspections will permit you to evaluate which control practices are effective and which need to be modified.

Pest Management Alternatives

As previously discussed, IPM uses a combination of complementary strategies to effectively manage pest populations. The following paragraphs describe some of the pest management alternatives available to the turfgrass manager.

Cultural Methods

Cultural methods involve manipulating the environment to make it less suitable for pest survival. These measures are usually preventive and must be implemented before the insect reaches pest status.

Turfgrass Selection. Select turfgrass species or cultivars that are well-adapted to local soil and environmental conditions. Adapted turfgrasses are better able to tolerate stress and are less likely to be damaged by insects than nonadapted grasses. Further, a blend of improved adapted grasses will usually outperform a single cultivar. Information on locally adapted turfgrasses is available from many Extension offices, nurseries, and garden centers.

Planting insect-resistant turfgrasses is another valuable IPM tool. Resistance to insect pests has been found in many plants, although the degree of resistance may vary considerably from one species or cultivar to another. Several cultivars of billbug-resistant Kentucky bluegrass are commercially available.

Endophyte-Enhanced Resistance. Endophytes are organisms, typically bacteria or fungi, growing within a plant. Turfgrasses infected with endophytic fungi in the genus Acremonium have shown enhanced resistance to many insect species including aphids, leafhoppers, chinch bugs, armyworms, webworms, and billbugs. Among the turfgrasses containing endophytes are cultivars of perennial rye, and tall and fine fescues. Useful endophytes have not been found in Kentucky bluegrass, creeping bentgrass, or buffalograss.

Effective Maintenance. Many insect pests associated with turfgrasses are attracted to lush, overly maintained turf. Sound cultural practices which optimize plant health and vigor enable the turf to withstand higher pest infestation levels and recover more rapidly from insect and mite injury. Careful turfgrass management is one of the best insect prevention strategies available.

Biological Control

This important IPM strategy utilizes beneficial organisms including predators, parasites, or insect pathogens to reduce pest populations. It can be implemented by releasing beneficial organisms into the turf area, or by modifying cultural, chemical, and other control practices to conserve existing natural enemy populations. In general, effective use of this approach requires a detailed knowledge of predator/prey or parasite/host biology, accurate timing, and careful application procedures.

Beneficial Insects and Mites. Natural populations of predators (e.g. lady beetles, big-eyed bugs, ground beetles, lacewings, spiders, predaceous thrips, and mites) and parasites (e.g. parasitoid wasps, tachinid flies) are valuable in reducing infestations of insect and mite pests. When these or other beneficial organisms are observed in the turf, care should be taken to ensure their survival. If pest control becomes necessary, select corrective measures which minimize injury to beneficial organisms. Remember that a low level of pest infestation may need to be tolerated to attract and maintain natural enemy populations.

Disease-causing Microorganisms. Certain disease-causing organisms or their products also can be used to reduce insect populations. Among the microorganisms known to attack turfgrass insects are bacteria, fungi, viruses, protozoans, and nematodes. Products containing bacteria and nematodes are available through pest management supply companies and some pesticide manufacturers.

Bacteria. *Bacillus thuringiensis,* commonly called "B.t.," is marketed under a number of trade names. When certain species of insects ingest this common soil-inhabiting bacterium, a bacterial toxin acts upon the insect digestive tract causing the insect to stop feeding, sicken, and die within four to seven days. Until recently, control with this microbial insecticide was limited to caterpillars (e.g. cutworms and sod webworms), and mosquito and fungus gnat larvae. However, strains of *B. thuringiensis* may soon be available to control white grubs, billbugs, and eventually other insect pests.

One moderately successful microbial control program

employed in some parts of the United States, involves the use of *Bacillus popillae,* a commercially available bacterium that causes milky disease in Japanese beetle grubs. Unfortunately, this bacterium does not affect all species of white grubs (including the *Cyclocephala* and *Phyllophaga* grubs common to the Northern Great Plains). In addition, it takes several years to reduce grub populations, and can be adversely affected by certain pesticides. Milky disease is not considered useful for white grub control in the Northern Great Plains.

Nematodes. Several species of beneficial or entomo-pathogenic nematodes are mass produced and available from commercial suppliers. These nematodes enter the insect's body and release bacteria which kill the insect host. One nematode species, *Steinernema carpocapsae,* is reasonably effective for control of sod webworms, armyworms, and cutworms, particularly if applied when the worms are small. It also shows promise for controlling bluegrass billbugs, but seems to have little activity against white grubs. Other nematode species under development provide much higher levels of white grub control.

Natural enemies

Beneficial insects reduce the numbers of pests damaging turf. Correctly identifiying beneficial insects and using pest control measures which minimize injury to them is an important part of an integrated pest management program. If turf damage is evident, but no pests are present, look for beneficial insects which may be helping reduce pest populations.

Ground beetle.

Ground beetle larva.

Lady beetle.

Lacewing.

Big-eyed bug.

Damsel bug.

Wolf spider.

Ants preying on cricket.

Wasp parasites attacking aphids.

Wasp parasites on cutworm.

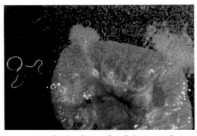

Nematode-infected white grub.

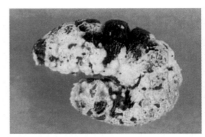

White grub infected with fungus.

Wildlife. Insect-eating birds and small mammals can be attracted to turf areas by planting trees and shrubs that provide cover and furnish berries for food. Birds also can be encouraged by providing water or nesting sites. It should be recognized, however, that some bird and animal species can be highly destructive to turfgrass, and may do more harm than good.

Insecticides/Acaricides

Insecticides and acaricides are the most powerful tools available for insect and mite control in turf. In many cases, they afford the only practical method of reducing pest populations that have already reached damaging levels. Insecticides have rapid corrective action in preventing further pest damage and offer a wide range of properties and application methods. They are relatively inexpensive and often result in substantial economic or aesthetic benefit. Some potential problems associated with insecticide use include the development of pest resistance, outbreaks of secondary pests, adverse effects on nontarget organisms including humans, pets, wildlife and beneficial insects, hazardous residues in our food supply, and ground water contamination.

When insecticides are used in an IPM program, they should be carefully selected and their application timed with respect to the developmental stages of the target pest. Insect monitoring information can help pinpoint the optimal time for treatment. Proper selection and timing of pesticide applications are extremely important in obtaining the best control with the least harm to the environment. Observe damage threshold levels (i.e. treat only when necessary) and limit treatments to infested areas whenever possible. Ensure proper calibration of the application equipment and always read, understand, and follow all label directions.

Insecticide Application Techniques

The following recommendations apply mainly to standard insecticide applications. Some biological control agents and new insecticides will require special handling and application techniques. Read the product label and discuss application procedures with the supplier before use.

For surface-active insects, the turf area should be mowed and the clippings removed prior to application to enhance insecticide penetration into the canopy. A thorough irrigation before application will move insects out of the thatch and soil and bring them to the surface. For night-feeding insects, apply the insecticide in the late afternoon or early evening. Light irrigation (1/8 inch) after treatment will rinse the insecticide off grass blades and into the turf. A heavier (1/4 inch) irrigation should follow granular applications to wash granules off grass blades and activate the insecticide.

In the case of soil-inhabiting insects, it is important that the insecticide move through the thatch layer and down to the root zone of the turf where the insects are feeding. Thatch layers of 1/2 inch or more can greatly reduce the effectiveness of an insecticide by intercepting and chemically binding the active ingredient. Reducing the thatch layer or aerating the turf prior to application increases insecticide efficacy.

For optimum control of soil-active insects, apply 1/2 inch of water 24 to 48 hours before the chemical application to encourage the insects to move closer to the surface and to decrease the absorbency of the thatch. This pretreatment irrigation is especially important if conditions have been hot and dry and insects are deeper in the soil. Immediately after the insecticide treatment, apply a heavier

irrigation of 3/4 to 1 inch to ensure effective thatch-soil penetration.

Always keep people and pets off treated areas until the spray has dried. Never allow sprays to puddle because honey bees and wildlife may be injured. Remember that it may take several days after treatment to achieve control of surface-active insects and longer for soil inhabitants.

Contact your local Extension office for a current list of registered insecticide products.

Major Insect and Mite Pests of Turfgrass

The following section provides descriptions, life histories, damage symptoms, sampling techniques, and management strategies for the major insect and mite pests of turfgrass in the Northern Great Plains. *A Key to Common Turfgrass Insects* and a pest occurrence chart, *Seasonal Activities of Major Turfgrass Pests*, with suggestions for sampling and timing treatments are provided on pages 73 and 76. The seasonal activity periods in the chart are approximations based on long-term averages. Actual activity periods can vary one to six weeks earlier or later than shown, depending on the season.

White Grubs

White grubs are the larval stage of a group of beetles collectively known as scarabs (family Scarabaeidae). While there are many species of scarab beetles in the Northern Great Plains, the larvae of only a relative few cause significant injury to turf. Among these are the masked chafers *Cyclocephala* spp. (annual white grubs), May/June beetles, *Phyllophaga* spp. (three-year grubs), the black turfgrass ataenius, *Ataenius spretulus,* and most recently the Japanese beetle, *Popillia japonica.*

White grubs.

Descriptions and Life Histories

All white grubs are similar in appearance with cream-colored, C-shaped bodies, reddish-brown heads and three pairs of short legs imme-diately behind the head. When fully developed, they range from 1/4 to 1/2 inch in length, depending on the species. Identification of the different groups of white grubs is possible by examining the arrangement of hairs and spines on the raster area on the underside of the termi-nal abdominal segments (*Figure 6*). These patterns can be distinguished using a small hand lens. The arrangement of hairs on masked chafer grubs is random with no clearly defined lines, while hairs on May/June beetle grubs are arranged in two distinct parallel lines. Japa-nese beetle grubs are charac-terized by a pattern of rastral

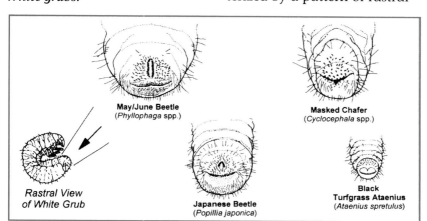

Figure 6. Raster patterns used to differentiate white grub species.

hairs arranged in a "V" shape, whereas the black turfgrass ataenius is distinguished by its small size and pad-like structures on the end of the abdomen.

Masked Chafer (Annual White Grubs)

Annual white grubs complete their life cycle in one year (*Figure 7*). Adults are tan, about 5/8 inch long, and have a dark, mask-like marking over the eyes. Adults are normally present from late June through July. They are highly attracted to lights and are frequently observed around windows or porch lights. Adult masked chafers do not injure turf or other vegetation.

Masked chafer beetles deposit eggs in the top 2 inches of soil, often in small clusters. Small grubs hatch during late July and early August and immediately begin feeding on grass roots. Most damage occurs in late summer and early fall after the grubs have reached the second and third larval stages. With the onset of cold weather, grubs move deeper in the soil to overwinter. As soil temperatures warm in the spring, they return to the root zone, feed for a brief period, pupate, and emerge as adults to begin a new cycle. Spring feeding is not as destructive to

Southern masked chafer.

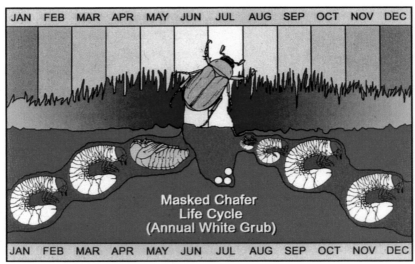

Figure 7. Life cycle of annual white grubs.

44

turf as late summer and fall feeding. Consequently, spring treatments are rarely required.

May/June Beetles (Three-Year Grubs)

Phyllophaga grubs require three years to complete their life cycle (*Figure 8*). Adult May/June beetles are larger than masked chafers (5/8 to 7/8 inch) and range in color from tan to brown to almost black. Adults emerge from the soil in May and June and fly around lights at night. While adults do not attack turf, they do feed on foliage of a wide range of trees, shrubs, and other plants. Eggs are deposited in the soil and hatch in

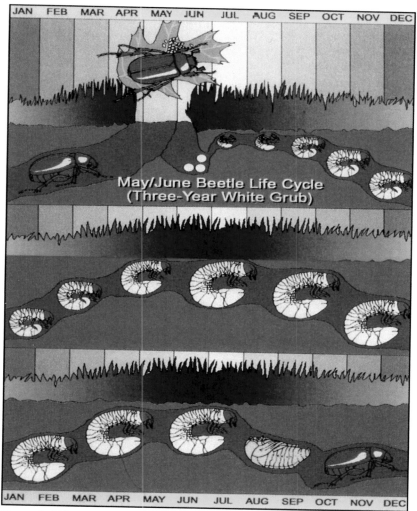

Figure 8. Life cycle of three-year grubs.

three to four weeks. Small grubs feed on grass roots during the first summer, moving down in the soil profile with the onset of cooler fall temperatures. Grubs return to the upper root zone in April or May, actively feed throughout the second growing season, then again move deeper in the soil to overwinter. In the third year, *Phyllophaga* grubs return to the root zone and feed until May or June, when they enter the pupal stage. Adults develop from the pupae late in the summer, but remain in the soil until the following May or June, completing their life cycle.

Black Turfgrass Ataenius

Black turfgrass ataenius adults are dark brown or black and about 1/4 inch long. Adults overwinter in loose soil, pine needles, and leaf litter and begin moving into turfgrass in March or April. Females deposit eggs in soil and thatch. Upon hatching, the larvae feed on grass

May/June beetle.

Black turfgrass ataenius.

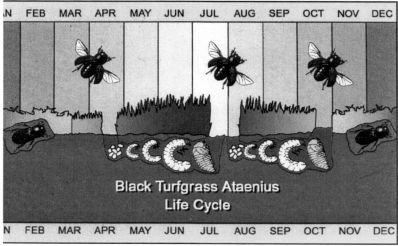

Figure 9. Life cycle of black turfgrass ataenius.

roots for three to five weeks before pupating. Most first-generation adults emerge in mid-July. Second generation larvae begin appearing in late July or early August and mature into the overwintering adults by October. Black turfgrass ataenius larvae are almost identical in appearance to other species of white grubs, but are much smaller (1/4 inch). Accordingly, larger numbers of these grubs must be present before severe turf injury occurs. Damage by this insect has primarily occurred on golf course fairways. The life cycle of the black turfgrass ataenius is depicted in *Figure 9.*

Japanese Beetle

Japanese beetles were introduced into the Northern Great Plains on infested nursery stock in the early 1980s. Japanese beetle larvae feed on the roots of a wide range of grasses and woody ornamentals and are one of the most destructive pests of turf, landscapes, and nursery stock in the northeastern United States. Japanese beetle adults are also voracious plant feeders and are capable of damaging the foliage, flowers, and fruit of nearly 300 plant species.

The occurrence, damage symptoms, and timing of treatment for the Japanese beetle are similar to those of the masked chafer (*Figure 10*).

Japanese beetle.

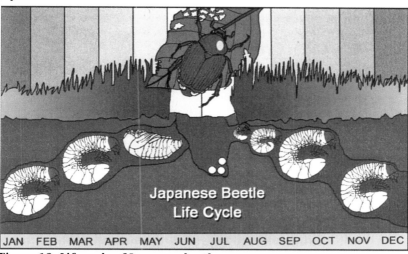

Japanese Beetle
Life Cycle

| JAN | FEB | MAR | APR | MAY | JUN | JUL | AUG | SEP | OCT | NOV | DEC |

47

Figure 10. Life cycle of Japanese beetle.

Adults are active from late June through early August. During daylight hours, they often feed in clusters on host plants such as apple, grape, rose, and linden. Eggs are deposited during July and early August with the majority of turf damage occurring in late summer and fall. Japanese beetle grubs overwinter below the frostline in the soil. There is a single generation each year.

Damage Symptoms

White grubs are among the most destructive insect pests of turfgrass. They feed below the soil surface on the roots and rhizomes of all commonly used turfgrass species and cultivars, and can eliminate the plant's entire root system. Where abundant, white grubs can destroy large areas of turf in a short time.

After hatching from eggs, white grubs begin feeding on the roots and underground stems of turfgrasses. The first evidence of injury is localized patches of pale, discolored and dying grass displaying symptoms of moisture stress. Damaged areas are small at first, but rapidly enlarge and coalesce as grubs grow and expand their feeding range. Turf in such areas will have a spongy feel under foot and can be easily lifted from the soil surface or rolled like a carpet, revealing the C-shaped

white grubs underneath. Damage is most apparent in mid-August through early September when white grub feeding activity is greatest.

Inadequate irrigation and drought stress may compound damage. Egg-laying females are generally attracted to vigorous, well-watered turf, and adequate moisture is essential for eggs to complete development. Once eggs have

Turf pulled back to reveal white grub damage.

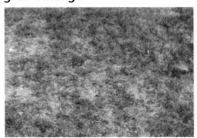

White grub damage.

Damage from animals foraging for white grubs.

hatched, however, white grubs will feed on either drought stressed or well-irrigated turf.

Several animals, especially skunks, raccoons, and moles, are highly attracted to turf insect infestations, and signs of their foraging in an area are strong indications of white grub activity. Flocks of birds, particularly starlings, feeding in the turf provide additional evidence of a possible infestation.

Sampling Techniques

Sampling for white grubs should begin early in the predicted grub activity period and before signs of injury are visible (once damage appears, considerable root injury will already be present). Since white grubs do not distribute themselves evenly throughout the turf, it is essential that the entire turfgrass area be sampled in a consistent, uniform pattern. Enough samples should be taken to assure a reasonably accurate estimate of white grub numbers in the sampled area. At each sample site, cut two 1/4 square foot (6" x 6") sections of turf on three sides, peel back the sod and examine the upper 2 inches of root zone for the presence of white grubs. Turfgrass managers with access to a golf course cup cutter can substitute 4-inch (0.1 square foot) diameter turf-soil core samples. If no white grubs are detected but damage is present, examine the turf for other causes of injury such as disease, excessive thatch, moisture stress, heat damage, and/or sod webworm or billbug feeding.

Management Strategies

In most years, the first week in August is the optimum time to control white grubs in turf — if sampling indicates that corrective measures are justified. At this time, most eggs should have hatched, and the small grubs will be feeding near the soil surface where they are more easily controlled. Damage from these grubs will not become apparent until later in the season when grubs are larger and the turf is stressed by hot,

Table 9. Treatment thresholds for white grubs.

Grub Species	Number per square foot	Number per 4-inch core
Masked Chafer	8-10	1
May/June Beetle	3-5	1
Black Turfgrass Ataenius	30-50	3-5
Japanese Beetle	8-10	1

dry weather. Treatments applied earlier in the season may be appropriate when using one of the newer longer residual insecticides.

Treatment Guidelines

The thresholds given in *Table 9* are estimates of the average number of white grubs necessary per unit area of turf to produce visible injury. They are provided to help turfgrass managers make treatment decisions. Remember that the condition of the turf, its value, and the damage caused by birds and animals searching for grubs, may alter these thresholds. In general, if white grub numbers exceed these thresholds in non-irrigated turf, an insecticide application is justified. Irrigated areas should be able to withstand substantially more white grub pressure before visual injury occurs. Treatment decisions should be based on average numbers of white grubs detected in the sampled area. If white grub numbers exceed threshold levels in only a few isolated patches, consider controlling these grubs with spot treatments.

Insecticidal Control

Effective chemical control of white grubs depends on moving the insecticide down to the root zone where grubs feed. This is best accomplished

by applying 1/2 to 3/4 inch of water immediately after application. Repeat irrigation every four or five days to continue moving the insecticide into the soil. This also keeps the crown and root area moist to encourage turf recovery. If conditions have been very hot and dry and grubs are deeper in the soil, a pretreatment irrigation of 1/2 inch applied 48 hours before the insecticide application should encourage grubs to move closer to the soil surface and enhance control.

Thatch plays an important role in reducing the efficacy of turf insecticides applied for white grub control. If the thatch layer exceeds 1/2 inch, a light aerification and increased post-treatment irrigation will enhance insecticide penetration and should improve control.

In many cases, some level of white grub activity will remain even after treatment. However, proper management should minimize damage from reduced infestations. Appropriate fertilization and watering to encourage a healthy turf will enable the grass to recover and reestablish in damaged areas. In some cases, a second insecticide application may be necessary to achieve an acceptable level of white grub control. This can be determined by resampling the area in question.

Billbugs

Billbugs have been reported as serious pests of lawns and other turf areas since the late 1800s. Today, we know of at least eight turfgrass-damaging species, the most important of which are the bluegrass billbug, *Sphenophorus parvulus*, the hunting billbug, *S. venatus*, and the "Denver" billbug, *S. cicatristriatus*.

Bluegrass billbug larvae.

Bluegrass billbug.

Descriptions and Life Histories

Billbug larvae (grubs) appear similar to white grubs but are legless. They have cream-colored bodies with brown heads, and when fully developed are about 1/4 to 1/2 inch long, depending on the species. Their bodies are slightly curved and resemble a grain of puffed rice.

Bluegrass Billbug

The bluegrass billbug was first reported as a turfgrass pest in Nebraska in 1890. Today, this insect is recognized as a serious pest of Kentucky bluegrass nearly everywhere the grass is grown. Although preferring Kentucky bluegrass (as its name implies), the bluegrass billbug also feeds on perennial ryegrass, fescue, and timothy grass.

Adult bluegrass billbugs are typical weevils (or snout beetles) with mouthparts located at the end of a curved snout or bill. These insects, which are about 1/4 inch long and dark brown to black, are slow moving and frequently "play possum" when disturbed. From April to June and again in September and October they can often be observed crawling on sidewalks and driveways near infested turf.

Hunting Billbug

The hunting billbug resembles the bluegrass billbug, but is slightly larger and has parenthesis-like markings on the back of the thorax. The grasses most seriously damaged by this billbug are zoysiagrass and bermudagrass, although injury to St. Augustinegrass and centipedegrass has occurred. Kentucky bluegrass is only occasionally damaged by this billbug species. The hunting billbug is a pest primarily in the southeastern United States, but is also found in mid-Atlantic states, and further west and north into Missouri, Kansas, and southeast Nebraska.

Denver Billbug

Comparatively little is known concerning the biology and life history of the Denver billbug. Damage from this insect has been reported in Colorado, Kansas, and western and central Nebraska. It is probably the most important billbug infesting Kentucky bluegrass lawns in Colorado and some areas of western Kansas and Nebraska. Adult Denver billbugs are considerably larger than either the bluegrass billbug or the hunting billbug, reaching 1/3 to 1/2 inch in length. This billbug can be differentiated from the other two species by

its larger size and the presence of distinctive, double-lobed markings on the wing covers.

Life Histories

Bluegrass and hunting billbugs typically have only a single generation each year, although a partial second generation of the bluegrass billbug has been reported in some areas. Both billbugs overwinter as adults in sheltered locations in and around infested turf. In southern states, hunting billbugs also may overwinter as larvae or pupae. The Denver billbug also overwinters as an adult, but is more likely to spend the winter as a mid-to-late-stage larva.

D. J. Shetlar, Ohio State University
Hunting billbug.

D. J. Shetlar, Ohio State University
Denver billbug.

Depending on springtime temperatures and geographic location, adult bluegrass and hunting billbugs become active in mid-to-late spring, with Denver billbug adults emerging a few weeks later (early May to June). After mating, females of all three species deposit their eggs in cavities chewed into plant stems near the crown. Newly hatched larvae feed for two to three weeks within stems before migrating to the crown and root zone of the plant and continue to feed on roots and underground stems. Billbug larvae usually feed just below the thatch layer, but are occasionally found as deep as 2 to 3 inches in the soil profile. When larval feeding is completed (mid-July for bluegrass and hunting

Billbug damage.

Billbug damage to lawn.

billbugs), pupation takes place in the soil or thatch. Adults begin to emerge in late July, feed for a brief period, then move to overwintering sites in leaf litter in protected areas such as hedges, tall grass, and around houses.

Damage Symptoms

The greatest injury from billbugs usually occurs from mid-June through late July during the period of maximum heat and drought stress. In areas where the Denver billbug is present, damage also occurs in the fall and early spring. Because billbug injury is easily mistaken for white grub or sod webworm damage, disease, or even plant stress, the damaged turf area should be carefully examined to confirm the presence of billbugs before making a management decision. Knowledge of prior billbug infestations in a turf area will be useful in making a diagnosis.

Newly hatched billbug larvae tunnel in grass stems, hollowing out the stem and leaving fine sawdust-like plant debris and excrement. Infested stems discolor and when pulled, readily break away at or near the crown. Subsurface feeding by older larvae can completely destroy the plant's root system, causing the turf to appear drought stressed. Under heavy billbug pressure the turfgrass will eventually turn brown and die. Adult billbugs also feed on grass stems and blades, but cause only minor injury to the turf. Billbug damage rarely occurs in turf stands less than three years old.

Sampling Techniques

Billbug adults are difficult to detect, even when numerous. The best time to begin monitoring is when adults are moving from overwintering sites back into turf areas. Look for bluegrass and hunting billbug adults on sidewalks and driveways from April through May, and Denver billbugs about one month later. Adults can be flushed from the turf by mixing 1 tablespoon of 1 percent pyrethrins or 1/4 cup of lemon-scented household detergent with 2 gallons of water and applying it over one square yard of surface area. These drenches irritate the billbugs and drive them to the surface in about 15 minutes where they can be counted.

Billbug larvae can be detected by selecting several locations in the turf area and peeling back 1/4 square foot (6" X 6") of turf to a depth of 2 to 3 inches at each site. Turfgrass managers with access to a golf course cup cutter can take 4-inch (0.1 square foot) turf-soil core samples.

Management Strategies

Effective cultural practices can significantly reduce billbug damage. Selection of adapted turfgrass cultivars and proper fertilization and irrigation programs will minimize the impact of billbug infestations. In addition, certain Kentucky bluegrass cultivars have natural resistance to billbugs, and several endophyte-enhanced, billbug-resistant cultivars of perennial ryegrass, tall and fineleaf fescues are now available. These have proven very effective in reducing billbug damage.

Insecticidal Control

The most reliable strategy for managing an established billbug infestation involves insecticide applications in late April through mid-May (approximately one month later for the Denver billbug) to reduce the number of overwintered adults before they can deposit their eggs. When attempting to control Denver billbug adults, additional treatments may be necessary to cover its extended egg-laying period. Experience has shown that an insecticide application is usually justified when visual observation or irritant flushes confirm the presence of **one adult billbug per square foot of turf**. If warranted, apply insecticides to newly mowed turfgrass (collect and remove clippings) and irrigate lightly after application to wash the insecticide off grass blades onto the soil surface where billbug adults are found.

Where pitfall traps are used **two to five adult bluegrass billbugs captured per trap** during the trapping period indicates the potential for light to moderate damage. If trap catches exceed **seven to ten billbugs per trap**, severe turfgrass injury is probable.

Insecticidal control of billbug larvae is difficult. Insecticides will not enter stems and may not penetrate the thatch layer to reach larvae feeding in the plant crown and root zone. During this period it may be better to water and fertilize damaged turf areas to stimulate new growth rather than to attempt control. However, if larvae exceed **25 to 30 per square foot of turf**, control is probably warranted. Before application, turf should be well-watered to moisten the

Constructing a pitfall trap

To construct a pitfall trap, use a large (16-ounce) plastic cup, and a 3-ounce collection cup. The cone-shaped cup is set into the 3-ounce collection cup, and both are inserted into the 16-ounce cup. The entire trap is placed into a hole made with a 4-inch golf course cup cutter. The trap should be situated so that the rim is slightly below soil level.

Traps should be set out in early April and placed at approximately 20-foot intervals in the vicinity of billbug "history" areas. Pitfall traps should be monitored one to two times a week until late May or early June (one month later for Denver billbug) when adult billbug activity is over for the season.

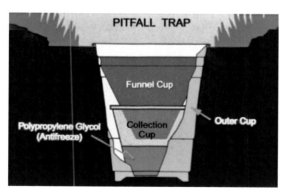

PITFALL TRAP

Funnel Cup

Polypropylene Glycol (Antifreeze)

Collection Cup

Outer Cup

Figure 11. Pitfall trap.

soil and enhance insecticide penetration. Immediately after treatment, heavy watering (1/2 to 1 inch) is needed to facilitate movement of the insecticide into the feeding zone. Aerification with irrigation may enhance larval control.

Sod Webworms

The sod webworm complex (family Pyralidae) is a large group of insects consisting of over 20 species that infest turfgrasses in the United States. Among the more important turfgrass-infesting species are those belonging to the genus *Crambus.*

Adult sod webworms, sometimes referred to as "lawn moths" are buff-colored, about 1/2 to 3/4 inch long with snout-like projections extending forward from the head. At rest, they fold their wings around the body, giving them a cylindrical or cigar-shaped appearance. Sod webworm larvae (caterpillars) are gray to tan with small dark spots on the body and brown heads.

They reach 3/4 to 1 inch when fully grown.

Life History

Sod webworms overwinter as partially grown larvae in silk-lined tunnels in the thatch and soil. In most years, larval activity resumes in April or early May. Webworms complete development, pupate and emerge as adults from mid-May to mid-June. Adult sod webworms rest in the turf and on shrubbery during the day and randomly scatter their eggs into the grass in the late afternoon and early evening while flying in a zigzag fashion just above the turf surface. Eggs hatch in about one week, and first-generation larvae feed

Sod webworm caterpillar.

Sod webworm adult.

Sod webworm damage.

until mid-summer. A second and partial third generation occur during the remainder of the season. Frequently, generations overlap with all stages present by late summer.

Damage Symptoms

Sod webworm moths do not damage turf. Larvae feed at night on grass leaves and stems near the soil surface, and hide during the day within burrows lined with silk webbing (hence the name "webworms") which penetrate through the thatch layer and into the soil. Sod webworms feed on most turfgrasses including bluegrass, bentgrass, tall and fine-leafed fescues, zoysiagrass, and buffalograss.

One of the first signs of webworm infestation is small, ragged brown spots in the turf. Upon closer inspection, these areas will have a grazed or scalped appearance. As webworms continue growth and feed, the injured areas enlarge and coalesce. Under heavy sod webworm pressure, large turf areas can be defoliated and even killed during heat and drought. While sod webworm larvae are active from early spring through fall, the most serious turfgrass injury usually occurs in mid to late summer.

Sampling Techniques

An early sign of potential infestation is sod webworm moths zig-zagging over the turf at dusk. If a sod webworm infestation is suspected, closely examine the turf for evidence of insect activity. Small patches of grass will be chewed off at ground level. Fresh clippings and green fecal pellets also are usually present. Examine the thatch layer and top inch of soil for larvae, silken tubes, and webbing.

To confirm the presence of webworms, mix 1 tablespoon of 1 percent pyrethrins or 1/4 cup of lemon-scented household detergent with 2 gallons of water. Mark off several 1-square-yard sections of the turf suspected of having a webworm infestation, and apply one gallon of the solution to each section. The solution irritates the caterpillars, causing them to move to the surface within 5 to 10 minutes where they can be counted.

Management Strategies

Sound cultural practices, especially proper irrigation, will usually allow turf to outgrow light to moderate webworm injury. However, if **15 or more webworm larvae are present per square yard** in reasonably healthy turf, an insecticide application may be justified. Fewer larvae can cause significant damage to stressed or less vigorous turf.

Insecticidal Control

If insecticides are used, the turf should be mowed and the clippings removed before treatment to enhance insecticide movement into the turf canopy. A thorough irrigation (1/2 to 3/4 inch) prior to application will move webworms closer to the surface. For best results, apply insecticides in the late afternoon or early evening when larvae are active. After application, lightly irrigate (1/8 inch), but delay heavy watering for 24 to 48 hours unless irrigation is indicated on the insecticide label. Granule applications also should be lightly irrigated immediately after application to wash granules off grass blades and activate the insecticide.

Cutworms and Armyworms

Cutworms and armyworms are the larvae (caterpillars) of several species of night-flying moths in the family Noctuidae. Caterpillars in this group are characterized by three pairs of legs situated behind the head, fleshy prolegs, and a distinct head. Adults (moths) are robust, drab-colored, and hairy with wingspans up to 1 1/2 inches

across. Typically, the front wings are darker than the hind wings and have various patterns of light and dark markings. Cutworm and armyworm larvae are only occasional pests of turfgrasses in the Northern Great Plains. Adults do no damage to turf.

Cutworms

The most common turf-infesting species of cutworms are the black cutworm, *Agrotis ipsilon*, variegated cutworm, *Peridroma saucia*, and bronzed cutworm, *Nephelodes minians*. Fully grown larvae reach 1 1/2 inches, with the bronzed cutworm being slightly larger. All species have a dark brown to gray head.

Black cutworm.

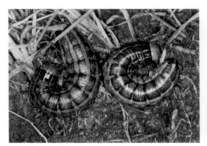

Bronzed cutworm.

Descriptions and Life Histories

The black cutworm is dark gray to black with a pale stripe down the back, but with few other distinguishing markings. Bronzed cutworms are dark brown to black on the upper side of the body and paler on the underside. The upper surface has three narrow yellow stripes and a broad white-yellow stripe running down each side. The entire body has a distinctive bronze sheen. The variegated cutworm is grey to brown with an orange lateral stripe and a series of darker lateral markings. A row of yellow or white dots runs down the middle of the back.

Life histories of the various cutworms differ depending on the species. The black cutworm does not overwinter in the Northern Great Plains. Moths migrate northward from southern states in early spring and deposit clusters of 10 to 20 eggs on grasses and weeds. Wind patterns (which affect the migration and ultimate distribution of the

moths) and local environmental conditions strongly influence the severity of black cutworm infestations. There may be as many as three generations per year. Bronzed cutworms overwinter as eggs which hatch in early spring. Fully grown larvae are present by late April and pupation occurs during mid-August. Bronzed cutworms have only a single generation each year. Variegated cutworms overwinter as partially grown larvae and resume feeding as grasses start to green up in the spring. Adults begin to appear in late spring and deposit up to 2000 eggs in clusters of 100 or more under the sheaths of grass blade. There are two to four generations of variegated cutworms each year.

Armyworms

The armyworm, *Pseudaletia unipuncta*, and fall armyworm, *Spodoptera frugiperda*, are generally considered minor pests, but they have the potential for explosive outbreaks in turfgrass.

Descriptions and Life Histories

Armyworms are 1 1/2 to 2 inches long at maturity and vary in color from gray to yellowish green tinged with pink. They have a narrow broken stripe down the center of the back and a lighter stripe

Variegated cutworm.

along each side. The head is light brown with a distinct honeycomb pattern. Armyworm adults are light reddish brown with a small white spot near the center of each forewing. The moths fly at night and are highly attracted to lights.

Fall armyworms are 1 1/2 to 2 inches long when fully grown and range in color from pink to yellow-green or gray to almost black. The fall army-worm has stripes on the body and an inverted white "Y" marking on the front of the head.

Armyworms and fall armyworms do not overwinter in the Northern Great Plains and must migrate northward from southern states in the spring. Females usually begin depositing their eggs on grasses in May. Larval feeding and migration typically occur at night with larvae hiding in the thatch during the day. Infestations of these insects are sporadic and occur only when egg-laying adults successfully migrate north. Armyworms complete two to three generations in the Midwest. The most serious turfgrass injury occurs in mid to late summer. The fall armyworm completes only a single generation each season in northern regions.

Damage Symptoms

Cutworms feed at night, cutting grass blades near the soil surface. Damage initially appears as small circular dead or dying spots that increase in size to 1 to 2 inches in diameter as the worms mature. Cutworms occasionally cause severe damage on golf course greens (especially bentgrass) where they live and feed around the openings made by aerification.

Armyworms also feed at night, and damage may occur before the larvae are detected. Grass blades that appear skeletonized are frequently an early sign of feeding activity by small larvae. Later, as catapillers mature, all above-ground plant parts are consumed. Areas that have been damaged by heavy infestations often appear closely

Armyworm.

Fall armyworm.

cropped in a circular pattern. Occasionally, large numbers of armyworms will develop in one area, then migrate to another after exhausting their food supply. This has been a problem in a few instances, when armyworms moved from maturing or recently harvested wheat fields into lawns, golf courses, cemeteries, sod farms, and other turf areas.

Sampling Techniques

Close examination of cutworm or armyworm-infested turf will reveal clipped or skeletonized grass blades mingled with green fecal

Cutworm damage to bentgrass.

Armyworm damage adjacent to wheat.

pellets. Larvae will be found near the edges of damaged areas. The presence of birds and/or animals foraging in turf areas is often an indication of cutworms and other surface-feeding insect pests.

To confirm the presence of cutworms or armyworms, apply 1 tablespoon of 1 percent pyrethrins or 1/4 cup of lemon-scented household detergent in two gallons of water over 1 square yard of turf. This irritates the caterpillars and forces them to the surface where they can be identified and counted. Scratching around in the thatch with a knife also may reveal their presence.

Management Strategies

Good cultural practices may allow a healthy, vigorous turf to withstand a moderate cutworm or armyworm infestation. In most cases, the turfgrass will outgrow the injury. Generally, it takes fewer caterpillars to damage mismanaged or stressed turf. Overgrown and lodged grass in the vicinity of the turf area creates an ideal environment for later cutworm or armyworm infestation.

Many natural factors help reduce cutworm and armyworm populations. When the weather is warm and humid, fungal diseases sometimes infect the insects, reducing infestation levels. In addition, several parasitic flies and wasps lay their eggs on cutworm and armyworm larvae. These caterpillars are later killed by the internal feeding of the parasites. Bird predation also can result in significant reduction of cutworm and armyworm populations.

Insecticidal Control

When natural enemies and cultural practices are not sufficient to prevent damage and cutworms or armyworms are present, insecticidal control may be warranted. For information on insecticide applications, refer to the section on Insecticidal Control under sod webworms.

Chinch Bugs

The two most important hemipteran (true bug) pests of turfgrasses in the Northern Great Plains are the chinch bug, *Blissus leucopterus leucopterus,* and a new species called the "buffalograss" chinch bug, *Blissus sp.* The "crops" chinch bug, known mainly for its damage to field crops, also feeds on a variety of turfgrasses, including Kentucky bluegrass, perennial ryegrass, fescue, bentgrass, and zoysiagrass. The buffalograss chinch bug however, has been observed only on buffalograss. Neither chinch bug species has been a major problem in the Northern Great Plains.

Description and Life History

The immature stages of both chinch bug species are similar in appearance. First instar nymphs are tiny (about 1/64 inch long), bright red insects with a white band across the abdomen. As nymphs mature (there are five nymphal stages), their color changes to orange-

Chinch bug adults and nymphs.

Buffalograss chinch bugs: long- and short-winged forms.

Chinch bug damage to buffalograss.

brown and finally to black. Adults are black and about 1/10 inch long (females are slightly larger than males). The adult "crops" chinch bug is black and white and has fully-developed wings which fold over the back and extend to the end of the abdomen. During most of the season, however, buffalograss chinch bug adults appear wingless, although very short "vestigial" wings are actually present. Flight activity is seldom observed.

Both species overwinter as adults in and around the turf area. In the early spring, adults emerge from overwintering sites and mate. Females insert their eggs behind leaf sheaths in the crown of plants and on underground roots in the surrounding soil. Eggs hatch during mid to late May. Nymphal development takes about a month. Adults of this first summer generation begin to appear in early July. All adult "crops" chinch bugs and a significant proportion of the buffalograss chinch bugs in this generation have fully developed wings and are capable of dispersing to new feeding sites. The second summer generation eggs hatch during mid to late July, and complete development in September and early October. Adults of this generation begin moving to overwintering sites with the onset of lower fall temperatures.

Damage Symptoms

Both nymph and adult chinch bugs feed by sucking juices from the leaves and stems of the turfgrass. During the feeding process, a salivary toxin is injected into the plant which disrupts the translocation of water and nutrients, resulting in wilt and discoloration of plant tissues.

Damage appears as patchy areas in the turf which turn yellow over time. As feeding progresses, the turf dries out and turns brown. At higher infestation levels, chinch bug feeding can result in severe thinning or even death of the turf stand. Damage is usually the heaviest in sunny locations during hot, dry periods and is often mistaken for drought stress.

Sampling Techniques

The most effective method of confirming a chinch bug infestation involves removing both ends from a two-pound (9-inch diameter) metal coffee can, pressing one end about 1 to 2 inches into the soil in an area of suspected infestation and filling the can with water. Chinch bugs will float to the surface in one to two minutes. Chinch bugs can also be detected by sprinkling 1/4 cup of lemon-scented household detergent mixed in two gallons of water over 1 square yard of turf and counting the insects as they crawl to the surface. Be certain that chinch bugs and not beneficial big-eyed bugs are being counted. Big-eyed bugs can be distinguished from chinch bugs by their gray to black oval bodies and large, conspicuous eyes.

Management Strategies

The best defense against chinch bugs involves the use of sound cultural practices designed to maintain turfgrass stands in optimum condition. Since these insects seem to prefer turf areas high in thatch and organic debris, cultural and mowing practices that minimize thatch accumulation should discourage initial invasion and may also help reduce chinch bug problems if and when they arise. Several turfgrass species and cultivars with natural or endophyte-enhanced resistance to chinch bugs are now available. These have proven very effective in reducing chinch bug damage. Information on adapted insect-resistant turfgrass species and cultivars can be obtained from your University Cooperative Extension office.

Insecticidal Control

If chinch bugs exceed **20 per square foot of turf (8 to 10 per 9-inch diameter cylinder)** and feeding damage is evident, control is probably justified. Before treatment, the turf should be mowed and the clippings removed. This will minimize interception of the insecticide by the turf canopy. Immediately following application, irrigate the treated area with 1/8 inch of water to wash the insecticide off grass blades and down into plant crowns and thatch where the chinch bugs are feeding. In turf stands where numbers are especially high, two insecticide applications may be required to achieve satisfactory control of both chinch bug generations. These treatments should be applied while chinch bugs are small. Normally this would be in mid-June for the first generation and late-July through mid-August for second-generation chinch bugs.

Greenbugs

The greenbug, *Schizaphis graminum*, a long-time pest of small grains and sorghum, has become a pest of Kentucky bluegrass turf in several midwestern states. While the greenbug is common throughout the Northern Great Plains, only rarely has it been a significant pest in turfgrasses.

Description and Life History

The greenbug is a light green aphid, about 1/10 inch long. It has a narrow, dark

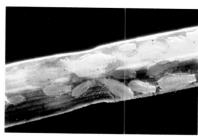
D. J. Shetlar, Ohio State University

Greenbugs.

green stripe down the back and black-tipped legs, antennae, and cornicles ("tail pipes"). There are both winged and wingless forms.

Greenbugs migrate to the Northern Great Plains from southern regions each year from April through June. Eggs hatch within the female aphid which then gives birth to live young. A single female can produce one to eight offspring each day for two to three weeks. Young aphids reach maturity in 6 to 10 days and begin to reproduce without mating. Depending on environmental conditions, from 12 to 20 generations can occur each season.

Damage Symptoms

Greenbugs feed by removing juices from plant tissues with piercing/sucking mouthparts. As they feed, greenbugs inject a potent salivary toxin which kills plant cells and causes discoloration of the leaf blades. Heavily infested plants turn yellow and may eventually die.

Circular patches of yellow to light-orange or dying turf may be an indication of greenbug infestation. If greenbugs are the problem, close examination of leaf blades should reveal colonies of feeding aphids. An infested grass blade may support 30 or more aphids. Concentrations of more than 3,000 greenbugs per square foot have been recorded.

Mild spring and summer weather facilitates greenbug survival and may result in damaging outbreaks. Infestations generally arise in shaded sites such as under trees or in the shadow of buildings, but may occur in sunny areas as well.

Sampling Techniques

Greenbugs can be detected by carefully inspecting grass blades for the presence of greenbug colonies or by sampling the turf with an insect sweeping net. The presence of lady beetles, lacewings, parasitic wasps, and other natural enemies that feed on aphids may also indicate a greenbug infestation.

Management Strategies

There are no established treatment threshold levels for greenbugs on turfgrass. However, if large numbers of greenbugs are present, and injury is increasing, an insecticide application may be warranted unless natural enemies are abundant. Apply a liquid insecticide to the greenbug infestation, including a 2- to 3-foot border around the damaged area. Thorough coverage is important. Do not irrigate for at least 24 hours after treatment.

Leafhoppers

Leafhoppers (Family Cicadellidae) represent a large family of insects which are usually more of a nuisance than injurious pests of turf.

Description and Life History

Leafhopper adults are wedge-shaped and vary in color from green to brown. They range from 1/8 to 3/8 inch in length. Immature leafhoppers are elongate, soft-bodied, and move rapidly, often sideways, over leaf blades and stems.

While many leafhopper species overwinter as adults or eggs in and around the turf area, others such as the potato leafhopper annually migrate from southern states to the Northern Great Plains in May and June. Depending on the species, there may be from two to three leafhopper generations during the season. In general, leafhoppers reach their highest population levels from mid summer through early fall.

Damage Symptoms

Leafhoppers feed by withdrawing juices from turfgrass leaves and stems. Initial injury appears as light-colored stippled areas on infested leaf blades. During the feeding process, the plant's vascular system is disrupted, which interferes with the translocation of water and nutrients and causes plant tissues to discolor and wilt.

Early leafhopper damage often appears as a graying or silvering of infested turf areas. As feeding and injury continues, the turf begins to dry out and gradually turns from yellow to brown. At very high infestation levels, leafhopper feeding can result in severe thinning or even death of the turf stand. Damage is usually the heaviest in sunny locations during hot, dry periods and is often mistaken for drought stress.

Leafhopper on buffalograss.

Sampling Techniques

Leafhoppers can be detected through visual observation or by sampling the suspected infestation with an insect sweeping net. When walking through the grass, look for the presence of flying adults. Also, an abundance of lady beetles, big-eyed bugs, parasitic wasps, and other natural enemies may indicate a leafhopper infestation.

Management Strategies

There are no established treatment threshold levels for leafhoppers on turfgrass. However, if leafhoppers are present in large enough numbers to be a nuisance, or if injury appears, an insecticide application may be warranted. Apply a liquid insecticide to the infested area (thorough coverage is important) and do not irrigate for at least 24 hours after treatment. Multiple applications may be needed throughout the season

Twospotted spider mite (left) and banks grass mite (right).

because of continuous reinfestation from adjacent turf or outlying areas.

Spider Mites

Several species of spider mites (Family Tetranychidae) are occasional pests of turfgrasses in Nebraska. Among the more important are the twospotted spider mite, *Tetranychus urticae*, Banks grass mite, *Oligonychus pratensis*, clover mite, *Bryobia praetiosa*, and winter grain mite, Penthaleus major. Spider mites are not insects, but are more closely related to spiders and ticks. While some spider mite species such as the Banks grass mite feed almost exclusively on grasses, others, including the twospotted spider mite, also feed on broad-leaved plants and conifers.

Twospotted Spider Mite and Banks Grass Mite

Twospotted spider and Banks grass mites are similar in appearance. They are tiny (less than 1/32 inch), oval-shaped, and range in color from green, yellow, reddish-brown to almost black. Males are slightly smaller and less rounded than females. Eggs are spherical and initially transparent, but darken before hatching.

Twospotted spider and Banks grass mites overwinter

as adult females and nymphs. Activity resumes as temperatures begin to warm in the spring. Eggs are deposited on the stems and foliage of the turfgrass. Upon hatching, mites pass through several developmental stages. First-stage larvae have six legs, whereas successive nymphal stages and adults have eight legs. These spider mites feed in colonies within a network of fine webbing on undersides of leaves.

Early season spider mite infestations are typically found on grass blades, but spread to other parts of the plant as mites increase in abundance. All life stages of the mites may be present at any given time, and there can be 7 to 10 generations during the growing season. Twospotted spider and Banks grass mites reproduce very rapidly under hot, dry conditions and can reach extremely high population levels, especially late in the summer.

Clover Mite

Clover mite adults are similar in appearance to twospotted spider or Banks grass mites, but are larger, more reddish-brown in color and have front legs which are nearly twice as long as the hind legs. These mites spend the summer as reddish-colored eggs on the stems, bark, and twigs of herbaceous and woody plants, and in the cracks and crevices of buildings.

With the arrival of cooler late summer and fall temperatures, eggs hatch and immature mites move to nearby host plants where several generations are produced before the onset of winter. As colder temperatures approach, adult females migrate to sheltered areas where they continue to lay eggs until extreme cold forces

Clover mites.

Clover mite damage on fescue.

Winter grain mite.

them into dormancy for the winter. In the early spring, newly hatched immatures and overwintered adults return to plant hosts to feed and reproduce. Turfgrass areas adjacent to overwintering sites can be severely damaged or destroyed.

Winter Grain Mite

Adult winter grain mites are dark reddish-brown with two distinct white spots on the back. They have a lighter-colored area at the end of the abdomen and four pairs of orange legs. Immature mites are reddish-orange, but darken as they mature.

Winter grain mites oversummer as reddish-orange eggs attached to the stems and roots of turfgrass. Eggs hatch in October and young mites begin feeding on the grass foliage. The first generation is completed in mid to late November when adult females begin producing eggs of the next generation. These mites become inactive during episodes of extremely cold winter weather. Mites of the second generation are most active from late February through early April and can contribute to winter injury in turf. Upon maturity, second generation adult females produce eggs that oversummer. By mid to late April the mite population is in rapid decline.

Damage Symptoms

Spider mites injure turfgrasses by sucking plant juices from the outer cell layers of leaves and stems. Mite damage is characterized by general lack of plant vigor and a silvery or pale yellow discoloration on leaves. As damage progresses, grass blades gradually turn yellow, dry out, and die.

Twospotted spider and Banks grass mites feed in colonies within fine webbing on lower surfaces of the grass blades. Infestations are more common in areas associated with drought stress such as near buildings, especially on southern exposures, and along sidewalks, driveways, and parking lots.

Clover mites have a very broad host range including turfgrasses, clover, grassy and broadleaf weeds, and some ornamental shrubs. While clover mites occasionally cause significant injury to turfgrasses, they are more often a nuisance when they invade homes and other structures in the fall and spring.

Winter grain mites are most abundant during the winter and early spring months and can be observed on sunny days in the thatch and crowns of the grass plants. In many cases, winter grain mite damage, when observed in the spring, is mistaken for weather effects. Winter grain mites seem to prefer Kentucky bluegrass and bentgrass, but will also readily feed on certain fescue cultivars.

Sampling Techniques

Begin sampling for twospotted spider or Banks grass mites in early summer and continue on a regular basis through early fall. Inspect turf stands, nearby vegetation, and the sides of buildings for the presence of clover mites in early fall and again in the early spring. Winter grain mite surveys should be conducted from late November through mid March. Spider mites can be detected by carefully inspecting thatch and grass blades with a 10X hand lens or magnifier for foraging clover and winter grain mites, or for colonies of twospotted and Banks grass mites on the undersides of leaves.

Management Strategies

Twospotted spider and Banks grass mites are difficult to control because they reproduce rapidly, especially in warm, dry conditions. In addition, some populations may be resistant to available pesticides. Infestations can often be reduced by irrigating the turf to disrupt mite colonies and to reduce moisture stress on the turf. If insecticides

are used, it is important to treat twospotted spider and Banks grass mites while colonies are small. Additional treatments may be necessary at 10- to 14-day intervals to prevent mite resurgence. For all spider mite species, apply a liquid insecticide to the infested area (thorough coverage is important) and withhold irrigation for at least 24 hours after treatment. Insecticides/acaricides are normally applied for winter grain mites in mid March to early April.

Clover mites inside homes and buildings can be collected with a vacuum sweeper (discard the vacuum bag and/ or its contents after collection) or sprayed with a household aerosol insecticide. When crushed, clover mites often leave a reddish brown stain, so care should be taken in their removal. Outdoors, the foundation and the surrounding 15 to 20 feet of turf can be treated with an insecticide to reduce mite numbers. Preparing an 18- to 24-inch wide strip around the foundation, cleared of vegetation and planted to plant varieties that are not attractive to the mites, should also help reduce invasions of these pests. Examples of flowers that can be used are zinnia, salvia, rose, chrysanthemum and petunia. Shrubs such as juniper, spruce, arborvitae and yew can also be planted, but are subject to infestation by other mite species.

Ants

Ants (Family Formicidae) are social insects which build their nests in soil, wood, or other suitable substrates. They occasionally become a problem in turf when they invade lawns, parks, golf courses, playgrounds, cemeteries, and other turfgrass areas. Ant mounds can be particularly troublesome on golf greens and fairways where maintaining a uniform playing surface is essential.

Field ants.

Ant mounds in turf.

Description and Life History

A typical ant colony consists of an egg-laying queen, males, immatures (eggs, larvae, and pupae), and hundreds to thousands of sterile female workers which can become a nuisance as they forage around buildings, sidewalks, foundations, and driveways. Ants consume a wide variety of foods including seeds, small insects, plant sap, flower nectar, and fungal growth. Many ant species feed on honeydew, a sweet liquid secreted by plant-feeding insects such as aphids, mealy-bugs, scale insects, and leafhoppers. In the spring and fall, colonies produce winged ants that leave the colony, mate, and seek new nesting sites.

Damage Symptoms

Ants normally establish their colonies in sunny loca-tions in well-drained soils. In turf, a nest consists of a series of underground tunnels and galleries which may extend three or more feet beneath the soil surface. Multiple openings provide access to the surface. During nest construction, ants excavate large quantities of soil which they deposit in mounds on the surface. Not only are these mounds un-sightly, but they can smother the turfgrass immediately surrounding colony openings and make routine maintenance difficult by producing a bumpy, uneven turf. Beneath the surface, soil excavations allow grass roots to dry, which can injure the turf stand. In addition, some ant species such as yellow ants and cornfield ants nurture colonies of root-feeding aphids which they "milk" for their honeydew. These aphids can further stress the turf by withdrawing sap from the roots and underground stems. In newly seeded areas, ants occasionally become a problem when they collect seeds and carry them back to the colony for later consumption.

Sampling Techniques

Ants are best detected by inspecting turf areas for mounds and worker ant activity. They also can be detected by sprinkling 1/4 cup of lemon-scented household detergent mixed in two gallons of water over 1 square yard of turf and observing the insects as they move to the surface.

Management Strategies

Effective ant control normally requires destruction of the queen. In most cases, this necessitates one or more applications of a liquid or granular insecticide. When a few colonies are present, apply insecticides directly to colony openings and the areas immediately surrounding the mounds. If colonies are numerous, broadcast treatments over the entire infested area may be the most practical solution. When liquid insecticides are used, apply sufficient spray volume to ensure thorough wetting of the soil surface. For granular applications, irrigate thoroughly after treatment to activate granules and move the insecticide down into the soil profile. In most cases, a single insecticide application will provide acceptable ant control for the season. Additional treatments may be needed if the queen was not eliminated or if ants recolonize the treated area. In addition to standard liquid and granular insecticides there are several bait formulations that can be placed in areas where worker activity is observed.

Table 10. Insects and Mites of Turfgrasses

Subsurface Feeders
- May or June beetle (3-year white grubs), *Phyllophaga* sp.
- Masked chafer (annual white grub), *Cyclocephala* sp.
- Black turfgrass ataenius, *Ataenius spretulus*
- Japanese beetle, *Popillia japonica*
- Bluegrass billbug, *Sphenophorus cicatristriatus*
- Hunting billbug, *Sphenophorus venatus*

Surface Feeders — Chewing
- Sod webworm, *Crambus sp.*
- Armyworm, *Pseudaletia unipuncta*
- Fall armyworm, *Spodoptera frugiperda*
- Cutworm — Family Noctuidae

Surface Feeders — Sucking
- Chinch bugs, *Blissus* spp.
- Greenbugs, *Schizaphis graminum*
- Spider mites — Family Tetranychidae
- Clover mites, *Bryobia praetiosa*
- Winter grain mites, *Penthaleus major*

Nuisance Pests
- Leafhoppers — Family *Cicadellidae*
- Ants — Family *Formicidae*
- Centipedes and Millipedes-Chilopoda and Diplopoda
- Wireworms — Family *Elateridae*
- Cicada killers, *Sphecius speciosus*

Beneficial Insects
- Big-eyed bugs, *Geocoris* sp.
- Ground beetles — Family Carabidae
- Lady beetles — Family Coccinellidae
- Lacewings — Family Chrysopidae

Table 11. Key to Common Turfgrass Insects

Soil-Active Insects Feeding on Crowns, Roots, and Underground Stems

1. C-shaped, cream-colored bodies; three pairs of short legs behind reddish-brown head; 1/4 to 1 inch in length..........................**White Grubs**

    a. Spines on raster without distinct pattern .... **Masked Chafer Grubs**

    b. Spines on raster arranged in two distinct parallel lines................................ **May/June Beetle Grubs**

    c. Spines on raster forming "V" shape .... **Japanese Beetle Grubs**

    d. Very small grubs; spines on raster without distinct pattern; two pad-like structures on raster........................**Black Turfgrass Ataenius Grubs**

2. Cream-colored, legless bodies with brown heads 1/4 to 1/2 inch long; appear similar to a grain of puffed rice .... **Billbug Larvae (Grubs)**

Surface-Active Insects Feeding on Leaves and Stems

1. Gray to tan caterpillars; 1/4-1 inch long with small dark spots on body.. **Sod Webworms**

2. Caterpillars with six true legs on front part of body; prolegs on abdomen; dark brown to gray head; 1 1/2 inches in length................. **Cutworms and Armyworms**

    a. Dark brown to black on upper side; paler on underside; three narrow yellow stripes on back and a broad yellow stripe on each side, bronze sheen... **Bronzed Cutworms**

    b. Dark gray to black with pale stripe down back; few other markings .... **Black Cutworms**

c. Gray to brown with orange lateral stripe and a series
    of darker lateral markings; row of yellow or white
    dots down middle of back ....**Variegated Cutworms**

d. Gray to yellow-green tinged with pink; stripes
    down center of back and along each side; head
    light brown with a distinct honeycomb
    pattern ....**Armyworms**

e. Gray to yellow-green; stripes on sides; inverted
    "Y" marking on head..............................**Fall Armyworms**

3. Hard shelled, dark brown to black; 1/4 to 3/8 inch
    long; weevils with mouthparts located at the end
    of curved snout or bill; slow moving, "play possum"
    when disturbed ....**Billbug Adults**

4. Predominantly black bodies with white wings or
    wingless; 1/10 inch; nymphs are small bright red
    with a white band across the abdomen..............**Chinch Bugs**

5. Light green aphid; 1/10 inch long; narrow, dark
    green stripe down back; black-tipped legs, antennae
    and cornicles ("tail pipes"); winged and wingless
    forms ....**Greenbugs**

6. Small, wedge-shaped green or brown bodies; 1/8 to 3/8
    inch long; very active — jumping, flying, or rapidly
    moving over leaf blades ....**Leafhoppers**

7. Minute (less than 1/32 inch), oval-shaped, reddish-
    brown to green bodies; often suspended in network
    of fine webbing on undersides of leaf blades.......**Spider Mites**

8. Small brown to black insects active on soil surface,
    which build volcano-like mounds of soil ....**Ants**

Turfgrass Weed Identification and Prevention

Roch E. Gaussoin
Extension Turfgrass Specialist
Alex R. Martin
Extension Weed Specialist

- Types of turfgrass weeds
- Identification keys and illustrations for major
  - grasses
  - sedges
  - broadleaf weeds
- Moss and algae
- Weed management

eeds are usually the most visible of turfgrass pests and are a major problem for turf managers and home owners. Weeds are a concern principally because they compete with desirable turfgrass plants for space, light, water, and nutrients. In addition, weeds detract from the appearance and function of turfs.

Any plant can be considered a weed if it's growing where it's not wanted. For example, although tall fescue is a major turfgrass species, it is considered a weed if it infests Kentucky bluegrass.

Management and control measures will vary depending on which weeds are present. Proper identification of the weed problem is the first step in developing a management strategy. This section provides a guide to identifying weeds which commonly infest turfgrass in the Northern Great Plains. Although the science of taxonomy relies on flowering or seed parts for plant identification, it's not difficult to identify weeds once the key vegetative features of each plant are known.

Weed illustrations by Jim Converse, provided courtesy of O.M. Scotts and Sons Company.

Types of Turfgrass Weeds

There are three types of weeds: grasses, broadleaves, and sedges.

Grasses have leaves with veins that run parallel to each other and are two-ranked (on opposite sides of the stem). The stem is jointed and hollow and the root system is fibrous. Examples include crabgrass, goosegrass, and foxtail.

Broadleaf weeds have leaves with a network of veins which are divided, and generally have a solid stem and main root system. Flowers are usually conspicuous. Dandelion, prostrate spurge, and ground ivy are examples.

Sedges closely resemble grasses in that the leaves have parallel veins. The main difference is that the stem is triangular, solid, and without nodes. In addition the leaves are three-ranked — arising from each side of the stem. Yellow nutsedge is an example.

Classification

Annuals, Biennials, Perennials

Weeds are often grouped by life span. Determining a weed's life span can be important when developing a management strategy. Weeds are classified as annuals, biennials, and perennials.

Annuals have a one-year life cycle. They germinate from seed, mature, and produce seed for the next generation in less than 12 months. Crabgrass, common chickweed, and prostrate knotweed are examples.

Biennials require two years to complete their life cycle. They form a rosette the first year, then flower and die during the second year. Many thistles are biennials.

Perennials are plants which live for more than two years, and may live indefinitely. Most perennials grow from seed, but may rise from reproductive structures such as tubers and rhizomes. Examples include dandelion, quackgrass, and yellow nutsedge.

Cool Season, Warm Season

Weeds can be further classified as cool season or warm season, based on when they germinate or grow most actively.

Cool season plants include winter annuals, cool season annuals, and perennials. Winter annuals germinate in the fall, overwinter, then produce seed and die the following summer. Common chickweed, henbit, and pennycress are examples. Cool season annuals germinate early in the spring and include prostrate knotweed and kochia. Cool season

perennials grow best during cool periods and go dormant during the hottest part of summer. Dandelion, rough bluegrass, and white clover are cool season perennials.

Warm season plants include both annuals and perennials. Warm season annuals won't germinate until soil temperatures warm up in May or June. Warm season annuals include prostrate spurge, purslane, and crabgrass. Warm season perennials remain dormant until June and go dormant again after the first frost. Nimblewill is an example.

Major Features in Monocot (Grass) Identification

Vernation is the arrangement of a leaf or leaves in the budshoot. In general, vernation can be classified as rolled or folded. For example, new shoots of Kentucky bluegrass are folded while new shoots of bentgrass are rolled.

Ligule refers to the structure which clasps the stem at the junction of blade and sheath. The type (membranous or hairy) and shape (tall, short, jagged, etc.) usually remains fairly uniform within each species.

Collar is the area on the outer side of the leaf where the blade and sheath join. It is generally much lighter in color and varies in size and shape from species to species.

Auricles are appendages that project from either side of the collar. They may be claw-like, long, or short. In quackgrass, slender auricles clasp the stem.

Sheath refers to the tubular leaf portion which wraps around or encloses the stem.

Edges of the sheath may join, overlap, or be closed. The sheath may be rough or smooth, cylindrical or flattened, or even compressed.

Blade is the upper portion of the leaf, which is divided from the sheath by the collar and ligule. The length, width,

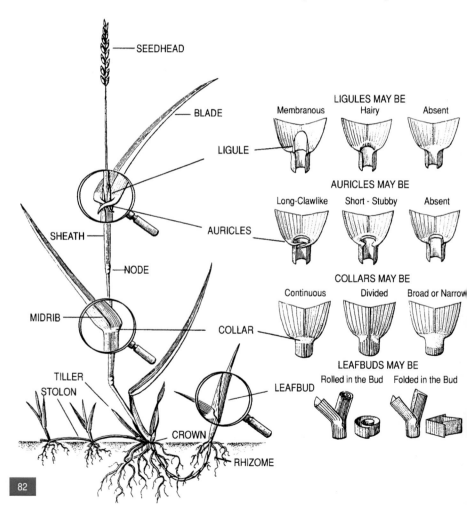

Figure 13. Parts of a grass plant.

type of tip, roughness, or smoothness are a few characteristics of various species.

Rhizomes are underground stems that produce new plants. A plant may have strong or weak rhizomes.

Stolons are horizontal above-ground stems that take root at various intervals, giving rise to new plants.

Seedhead is the collection of flower or seeding parts which are arranged in various ways (spike, panicle, etc.). It is an important identifying feature.

Spikelet is the unit of the seedhead which composes the seeding parts. Properly dissected and analyzed, it provides the most accurate method for identifying various species.

Other characteristics, such as growth habit and color, will help to identify the various grasses. To make identification even more practical, use a small magnifying glass to observe tiny parts. Magnification from 10x to 16x is ideal.

Panicle. Triangular in outline with seeding branches around the main stem. Examples: Bluegrass, Redtop.

Forming clusters of seeds. Examples: Bluegrass, Ryegrass.

Spike. Spikelets attached at the top of an unbranched stem. Examples: Timothy, Foxtail.

With long pointed awns.. Examples: Nimblewill, Wild Oats.

Slender seeding spikes attached at the top of the main stem. Examples: Crabgrass, Goosegrass.

Born singly on short branches. Examples: Witchgrass, Fall Panicum.

Slender seeding spikes attached along the top of the main stem. Examples: Signalgrass, Dallisgrass.

Containing several seeds. Examples: Sandbur, Buffalograss.

83

Figure 14. Parts of a grass plant seedhead.

Grasses

Annual Bluegrass (*Poa annua*)

Other Names: Poa, Winter-grass

Life Span: Cool season winter annual (subspecies exist which act as short-lived perennials)

Description: Annual bluegrass is a light green bunch-type grass. The leaf blades are soft, "V"-shaped, folded in the bud, and boat-shaped at the tip. The ligule is long, pointed, and membranous. Auricles are absent. The root system is fibrous and does not have rhizomes. Annual bluegrass grows low and is capable of producing seed heads at mowing heights lower than 1/4 inch. Growth from seed starts in early fall and often continues through the winter. This grass thrives in cool, moist conditions and may die suddenly during hot weather.

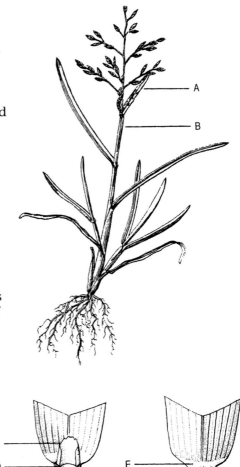

Figure 15. Annual bluegrass (*Poa annua*).
A. Blade: folded in the bud, soft, glossy, light green with boatshaped tips, 1/8 inch wide.
B. Sheath: compressed, smooth.
C. Ligule: medium long, acute, white, membranous.
D. Auricles: none.
E. Collar: narrow and continuous.

Rough Bluegrass (*Poa trivialis*)

Other Names: Roughstalked Bluegrass, Rough Meadow-grass, Birdgrass

Life Span: Cool season perennial

Description: Rough bluegrass is a light green to yellow-green stoloniferous grass. The leaf blades are soft, "V"-shaped, folded in the bud, and boat shaped at the tip. The ligule is membranous, long, pointed, and toothed near the tip. Auricles are absent. Collar is broad, smooth, and divided. Sheath is compressed, rough to the touch, and can be green or purple. The root system is fibrous. Rough bluegrass has become a weed problem in Kentucky bluegrass turfs due to seed contamination. In cool, wet springs rough bluegrass stolons from a single plant can spread 2-3 feet, giving the turf a patchy appearance. Rough bluegrass thrives in cool, moist conditions but often will go dormant and turn brown in summer.

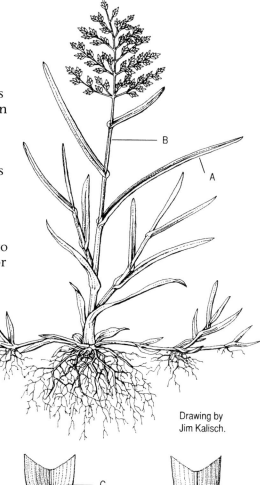

Drawing by Jim Kalisch.

Figure 16. Rough bluegrass (*Poa trivialis*).
A. Blade: soft, U-shaped, folded in the bud, boat-shaped at the tip.
B. Sheath: compressed, rough, green or purple.
C. Ligule: membranous, long, pointed, toothed near the tip.
D. Auricles: none.
E. Collar: broad, smooth, divided.

Large Crabgrass (*Digitaria sanguinalis*)

Other Names: Hairy Crabgrass

Life Span: Warm season annual

Description: Large crabgrass is light green and tillers profusely. The leaf blades are rolled in the bud, hairy on both sides, about 1/4-inch wide, and taper to a point. The ligule is membranous and long, with toothed margins. Auricles are absent. The sheath is hairy and split. The root system is fibrous and dense. The seed head is divided into finger-like segments. The stem grows prostrate and sends down roots where the nodes come in contact with the soil. As a result of tillering, one plant may take up an area 6 inches in diameter. Large crabgrass germinates when soil temperatures reach 55° to 60°F. Large crabgrass establishment is favored by low mowing heights and light, frequent irrigation.

Smooth Crabgrass (*Digitaria ischaemum*)

Other Names: Small crabgrass

Life Span: Warm season annual

Description: Smooth crabgrass is light green and tillers profusely. The leaf blades are rolled in the bud, sparsely hairy near the ligule, about 1/4-inch wide, and taper to a point. The ligule is membranous and long, with smooth margins. Auricles are absent. The sheath is smooth, split, and turns purple toward the fall. The root system is fibrous and dense. The seed head is divided into finger-like segments. The stems grow prostrate and send down roots where the nodes contact the soil. As a result of tillering, one plant may take up an area 6 inches in diameter. Smooth crabgrass germinates when soil temperatures reach 55° to 60°F. Smooth crabgrass establishment is favored by low mowing heights and light, frequent irrigation.

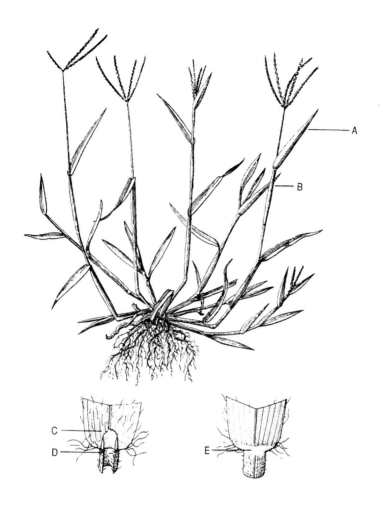

Figure 17. Crabgrass (*Digitaria sanguinalis*).
A. Blade: rolled in the bud, sparsely hairy, about 1/4 inch wide.
B. Sheath: compressed, hairy.
C. Ligule: long, acute, membranous, toothed.
D. Auricles: none.
E. Collar: broad, sparsely hairy.

Goosegrass (*Eleusine indica*)

Other Names: Silver Crabgrass

Life Span: Warm season annual

Description: Goosegrass has dark green leaves with stems which become white toward the base. The leaf blades are folded in the bud, about 1/4-inch wide, and taper to a point. The ligule is membranous, toothed, and divided at the mid-rib. Auricles are absent. The sheath is light green above and becomes white near the base. The sheath is flattened, with a few long white hairs near the collar. The root system is shallow and fibrous. The seed head is divided into finger-like segments, but thicker and more robust than crabgrass. The stems are thick and grow prostrate with several basal tillers radiating from a common point. Goosegrass germinates later than crabgrass, requiring soil temperatures near 60°F to 70°F. Goosegrass establishment is favored by compacted soil conditions and thin, open turfs.

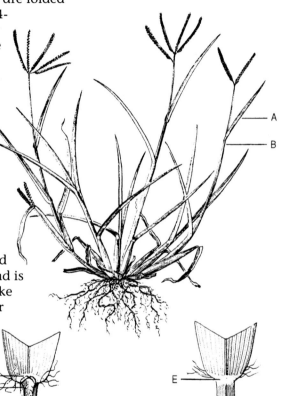

Figure 18. Goosegrass (*Eleusine indica*).
A. Blade: folded in the bud, rough texture, pointed, apple green, about 1/4 inch wide.
B. Sheath: wide near the ground, green above, tightly compressed, overlapping, sparsely hairy along margins.
C. Ligule: medium long, membranous, toothed, divided by mid-rib.
D. Auricles: none.
E. Collar: broad, continuous, hairy.

Yellow Foxtail (*Setaria glauca*)

Other Names: Pigeon grass

Life Span: Warm season annual

Description: Yellow foxtail is an erect, bunch-type grass. The leaf blades are rolled in the bud, keeled in the lower portions, with long cobwebby hairs on the upper surface near the base. The ligule is a fringe of short hairs. Auricles are absent. The sheath is smooth and flattened. The stem is erect, flattened, and slightly bent at the nodes. The root system is shallow and fibrous. The seed head is a single cylindrical, spike-like panicle. The stems grow erect. Yellow foxtail germination requires soil temperatures of 60° to 65°F. Yellow foxtail establishment is favored by thin open turfs.

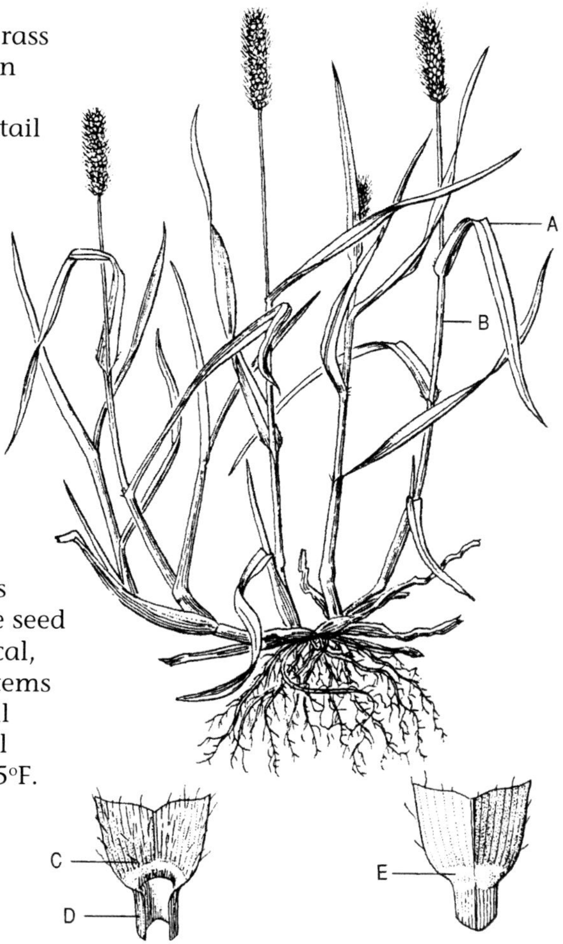

Figure 19. Yellow foxtail (*Setaria glauca*).
A. Blade: rolled in the bud, flat, often having a spiral twist, hairy on the upper surface near the base, about 1/4 inch wide or wider, sharp pointed.
B. Sheath: compressed, smooth, tinged with red.
C. Ligule: a fringe of short hairs.
D. Auricles: none.
E. Collar: broad, continuous, smooth.

Green Foxtail (*Setaria virida*)

Other Names: Pigeon grass

Life Span: Warm season annual

Description: The leaf blades are rolled in the bud and lack hairs. The ligule is a fringe of short hairs. Auricles are absent. The sheath is smooth and slightly flattened, with the margins distinctly hairy. The stem is erect, round, and smooth. The root system is shallow and fibrous. The seed head is a single cylindrical, spike-like panicle. The seeds produced are one-fourth the size of yellow foxtail. Green foxtail is a bunch type grass. Germination requires soil temperatures of 60° to 65°F. Green foxtail establishment is favored by thin, open turfs.

Stinkgrass (*Eragrostis cilianensis*)

Other Names: None

Life Span: Warm season annual

Description: Stinkgrass is a low-growing, bunch-type grass. The leaf blades are rolled in the bud, flat, dull green, tapered, and lack hairs. The ligule is a fringe of short hairs. Auricles are absent. The collar has long hairs at the edges. The sheath is slightly compressed. The stem is slender and smooth with a ring of glands at the nodes. The root system is shallow and fibrous. The seed head is a grayish-green panicle producing flat spikelets. Stinkgrass produces a disagreeable odor when crushed. Stinkgrass typically germinates later than most warm season grasses and can be troublesome when trying to establish new stands in mid to late summer. The seed head turns yellow when approaching maturity.

Figure 20. Stinkgrass (*Eragrostis cilianensis*).
Ligule: a fringe of hairs.
Auricles: none.
Collar: narrow, continuous, long hairs at the edges.

Sandbur (*Cenchrus pauciflorus*)

Other Names: None

Life Span: Warm season annual

Description: Sandbur is a low-growing grass that often forms mats. The leaf blades are folded in the bud, alternate, flat, narrow, tapered, and lack hairs. The ligule is a fringe of short hairs. Auricles are absent. The sheath is loose and flattened. The stem is smooth, branched, and flattened. The root system is fibrous. The seed head is a spike with 6 to 20 spiny burs which enclose the seed. Sandbur is a pale yellow grass which prefers dry, sandy sites and low maintenance turf. The spiny burs can cause painful injuries.

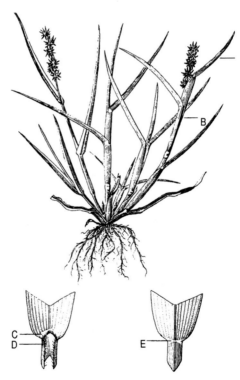

Figure 21. Sandbur (*Cenchrus pauciflorus*).
A. Blade: folded in the bud, few hairs near the ligule.
B. Sheath: loosely compressed, keeled, margins are hairy.
C. Ligule: short even fringe of hairs.
D. Auricles: none.
E. Collar: broad, continuous, sometimes with a few long hairs.

Tall Fescue (*Festuca arundinacea*)

Other Names: None

Life Span: Cool season perennial

Description: Tall fescue is a relatively coarse, bunch-type grass. The leaf blades are rolled in the bud, strongly veined on the upper surface, and rough along the edges. The ligule is membranous and short. Auricles are rudimentary. The lower portion of the stem is reddish purple, particularly in the spring and fall. The root system is mainly fibrous with rudimentary rhizomes. The seed head is an erect, somewhat compressed panicle. Tall fescue clumps are objectionable in fine textured turfs. Tall fescue has good heat and drought tolerance which allows this grass to invade drought stressed turfs. This coarse grass results in brown fibers on the leaf tips, especially if the mower is dull.

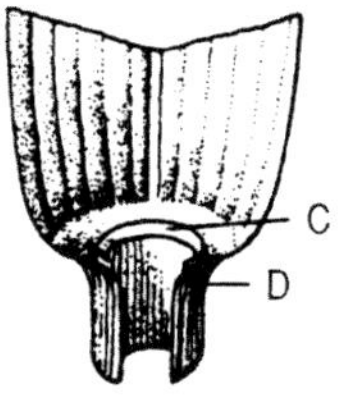

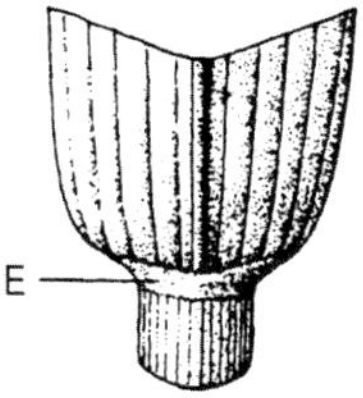

Figure 22. Tall fescue (*Festuca arundinacae*).
A. Blade: folded in the bud, glossy, rough on the margins, prominently veined on top surface.
B. Sheath: not compressed, reddish-pink near and below soil surface.
C. Ligule: very short, membranous.
D. Auricles: none.
E. Collar: broad, continuous.

Smooth Brome (*Bromus inermis*)

Other Names: None

Life Span: Cool season perennial

Description: The leaf blades are rolled in the bud, about 1/4- to 1/2-inch wide, tend to be lax, and often form a constriction which appears as an "M" or "W." The ligule is membranous and short. Auricles are absent. The lower portion of the stem is white with prominent veins. The root system is strongly rhizomitous. The seed head is an erect panicle, with branches in a circular pattern around the main stem. Smooth brome infestations usually result from lawns being started from pasture sod. Smooth brome starts growth early in the spring, slows during summer, and resumes growth in the fall.

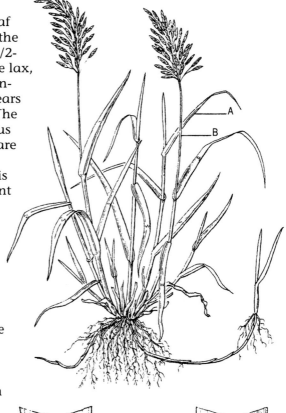

Figure 23. Smooth brome (*Bromus inermis*).
A. Blade: rolled in the bud, about 1/4 inch wide, smooth, often constricted to form an "M" or "W".
B. Sheath: not compressed, closed nearly to the top.
C. Ligule: short, membranous.
D. Auricles: none.
E. Collar: narrow, continuous.

Quackgrass (*Agropyron repens*)

Other Names: None

Life Span: Cool season perennial

Description: The leaf blades are rolled in the bud, flat, about 1/4 inch wide, lax, and rough on the upper surface. The ligule is membranous and short. Auricles are conspicuous, claw-like, and clasp around the stem. The lower portion of the sheath has short hairs. The stem is erect and branched at the crown. The root system is strongly rhizominous, being yellow or white and very extensive. Rings of fibrous root hairs occur every 3/4 to 1 inch along the rhizomes. The seed head is an erect spike, 2 to 5 inches long. It is not very heat tolerant and grows most vigorously during the early spring and fall.

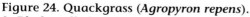

Figure 24. Quackgrass (*Agropyron repens*).
A. Blade: rolled in the bud, pale green, rough on upper surface, about 1/4 inch wide.
B. Sheath: not compressed, lower sheaths hairy, upper ones smooth.
C. Ligule: very short, membranous.
D. Auricles: claw-like, slender, clasping the stem.
E. Collar: broad, continuous.

95

Nimblewill
(*Muhlenbergia schreberi*)

Other Names: None

Life Span: Warm season perennial

Description: Nimblewill is a thin, wiry, pale green grass. The leaf blades are rolled in the bud, short, narrow, pointed, and grow at a 45-degree angle from the stem. The ligule is membranous, jagged, and short. Auricles are absent. Long hairs are present at the collar. The stems are slender, smooth, and decumbent. The root system is shallow and fibrous. Nimblewill spreads by short stolons. The seed head is a loose, spike-like panicle. Nimblewill forms circular patches as a result of its stoloniferous growth pattern. It is objectionable in cool season turfs because of its delayed greenup in the spring and early fall dormancy. It is usually found in shaded areas and drought-stressed turfs.

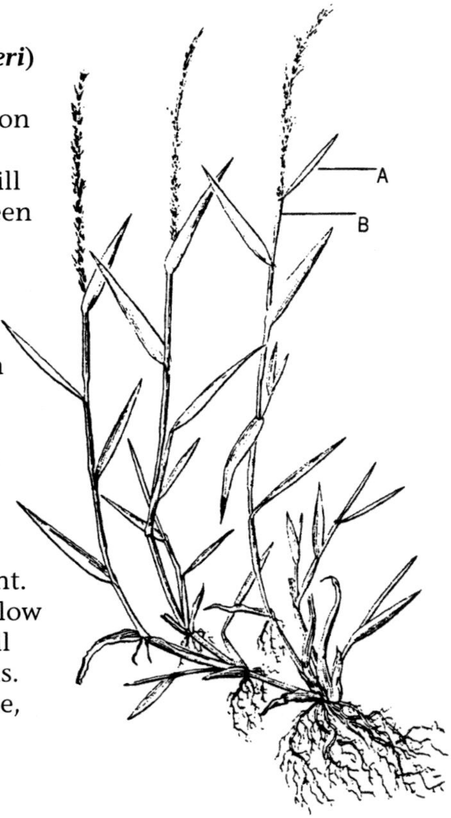

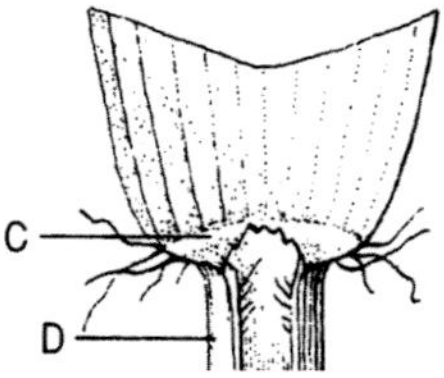

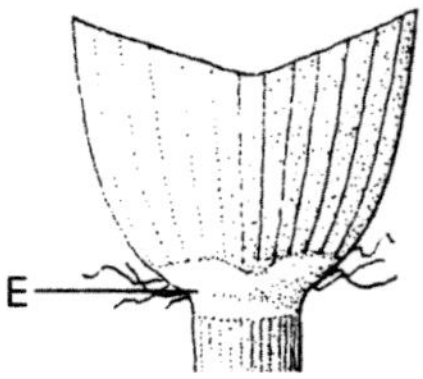

Figure 25. Nimblewill (*Muhlenbergia schreberi*).
A. Blade: rolled in the bud, short, pointed.
B. Sheath: compressed, white along margin.
C. Ligule: short, toothed, membranous.
D. Auricles: none.
E. Collar: continuous, broad, whitish, with marginal hairs.

Yellow Nutsedge (*Cyperus esculentus*)

Other Names: Nutgrass

Life Span: Warm season perennial

Description: Yellow nutsedge closely resembles a grass but is actually a sedge. The leaf blades are mostly basal, light green, "V"-shaped with a prominent mid rib, and three-ranked. The stem is triangular and erect. The root system consists of rhizomes which produce tubers. The seed head is surrounded by several leaves. The flowers are umbel and yellow or brown. Yellow nutsedge grows rapidly in July and August and generally prefers wet soil. Due to the root system and tubers, yellow nutsedge can spread rapidly throughout a lawn. The plant turns an objectionable brown toward fall.

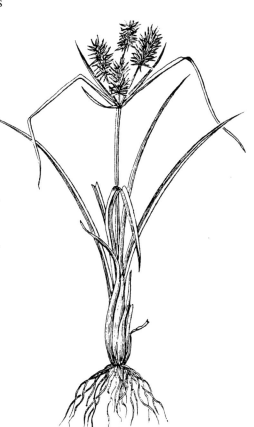

Figure 26. Sedge (many species). Blades: "V-shaped" in cross section, 8 to 10 inches long and tapering to a point, short, pointed. There are no auricles, collar, ligule, or sheath.

Broadleaf Weeds

Field Pennycress (*Thlaspi arvense*)

Other Names: None

Life Span: Winter annual

Description: Field pennycress resembles a mustard. The leaves at the base of the plant form a rosette and are petioled. The upper leaves clasp around the stem with ear-like projections, are alternate and toothed. The leaves produce a garlic odor when crushed. The stem is erect and smooth. Flowers are white with four petals. The seeds are contained in pods which are flat, circular, and broadly winged with a deep notch at the top. Field pennycress germinates in the fall, forms a rosette, and overwinters. Growth resumes early in the spring, at which time the plant bolts, producing flower stalks and setting seed by May. Field pennycress is most troublesome in fall- established lawns.

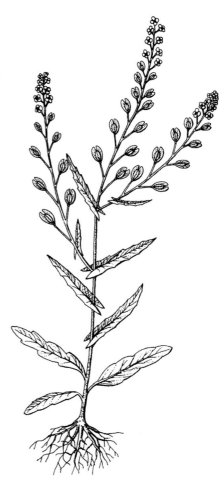

Drawing by Jim Kalisch.

Figure 27. Field pennycress (*Thlaspi arvense*).

Shepherdspurse (*Capsella bursa-pastoris*)

Other Names: None

Life Span: Winter annual

Description: Shepherdspurse resembles a mustard and can be confused with field penny-cress. The leaves at the base of the plant form a rosette and are coarsely lobed or toothed. The upper leaves resemble an arrowhead, and clasp around the stem with pointed lobes. The stem is erect and covered with coarse, gray hairs. Flowers are small, white with four petals, and in elongated racemes at the ends of branches. The seeds are contained in triangular pods. Shepherdspurse germinates in fall, forms a rosette and overwinters. Growth resumes early in the spring, when the plant bolts, producing flower stalks and setting seed by May. Shepherdspurse is most troublesome in fall-established lawns.

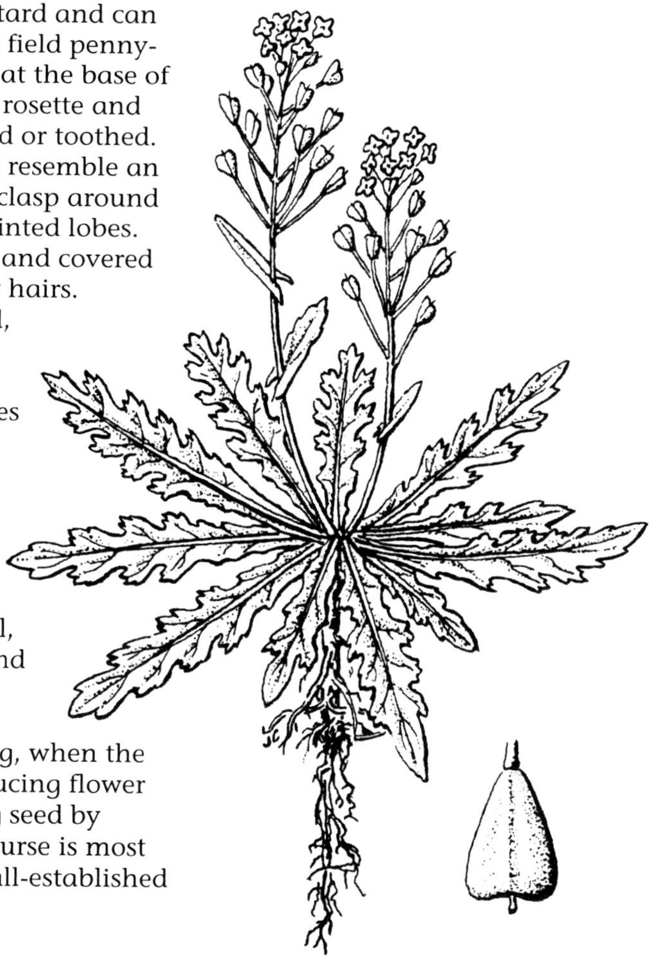

Figure 28. Shepherdspurse (*Capsella Bursa-pastoris*).

Common Chickweed (*Stellaria media*)

Other Names: None

Life Span: Winter annual, annual

Description: Common chickweed is a spreading, low growing plant. It is one of the first turf weeds observed in the spring. It thrives in cool, moist, shaded areas and disappears under high temperatures. In protected areas, it may occur all year. Chickweed germinates in fall or early spring, flowers most of the growing season, and produces seed. The leaves are opposite, oval-shaped, pointed at the tip, smooth, and shiny. The stems are multi-branched, weak, slender, and capable of rooting at the nodes. Flowers are small, white, and star-shaped with five notched petals. The roots are shallow and weak.

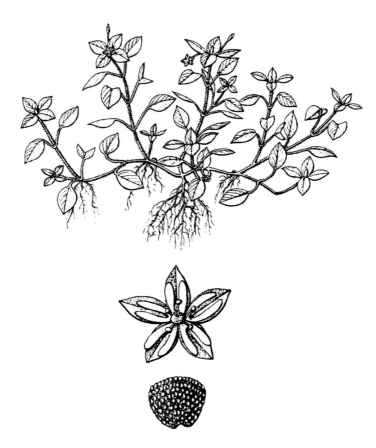

Figure 29. Common chickweed (*Stellaria media*).

Mouseear Chickweed (*Cerastium vulgatum*)

Other Names: None

Life Span: Cool season perennial

Description: Mouseear chickweed is a low growing plant which tolerates close mowing. The leaves are sessile, opposite, narrow, and hairy. The stems are hairy and root at the nodes. Flowers are small, white, and star-shaped with five notched petals. The roots are shallow and fibrous.

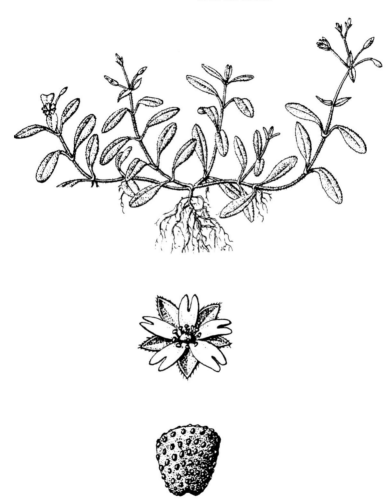

Figure 30. Mouseear chickweed (*Cerastium vulgatum*).

Black Medic (*Medicago lupulina*)

Other Names: Yellow Trefoil

Life Span: Warm season annual

Description: Black medic is a member of the legume family and can be confused with clovers. The dark green leaves alternate on the stem and each leaf consists of three leaflets. The leaflets are wedge-shaped with a small spur at the tip and prominent, parallel veins. The stems are prostrate, hairy, and rise from a crown area. The root consists of a strong taproot. Flowers are small, bright yellow compact clusters.

Figure 31. Black medic (*Medicago lupulina*).

White Clover (*Trifolium repens*)

Other Names: White Dutch Clover

Life Span: Cool season perennial

Description: White clover is a member of the legume family and can be confused with black medic. The dark green leaves alternate on the stem and each leaf consists of three leaflets. The leaflets have a white crescent-shaped mark and prominent, parallel veins. The stems are prostrate, hairy, and able to root at the nodes. This enables the plant to withstand close mowing. Flowers are white, sometimes with a tint of pink. White clover resumes growth early in the spring and goes dormant during hot weather, leaving objectionable brown areas in the turf.

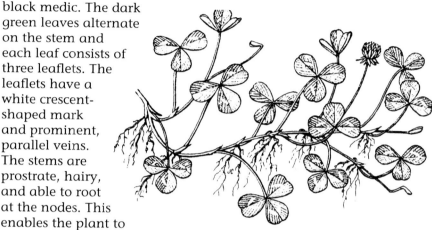

Figure 32. Clover (*Trifolium repens*).

Yellow Woodsorrel (*Oxalis stricta*)

Other Names: Oxalis

Life Span: Perennial/warm season annual

Description: Yellow woodsorrel can be confused with clover. The pale green leaves consist of three leaflets which are distinctly heart-shaped, and appear folded along the midrib. The branching stems are thin, sparsely hairy, and able to root at the nodes. The funnel-shaped flowers are small and yellow with five petals. As the flowers mature, a cylindrical seedpod is formed, which is five-sided and tapers to a point. Yellow woodsorrel is often found where the turf is thin or absent and grows from mid-spring to mid-fall.

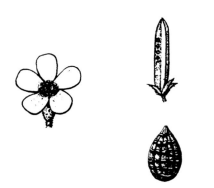

Figure 33. Yellow woodsorrel (*Oxalis stricta*).

Henbit (*Lamium amplexicaule*)

Other Names: None

Life Span: Winter annual/cool season annual

Description: Henbit is a member of the mint family, and is often confused with ground ivy. It is generally a problem in newly seeded turfs established in the fall. Henbit has a four-sided, square stem. The leaves are hairy, rounded, coarsely lobed, deeply veined, and are opposite. Toward the base of the stem, the leaves are long, petioled, and toward the top the leaves clasp the stem. The flowers are tubular or trumpet-shaped, pink or purple in color, and rise from the leaf axils. Henbit flowers in early spring.

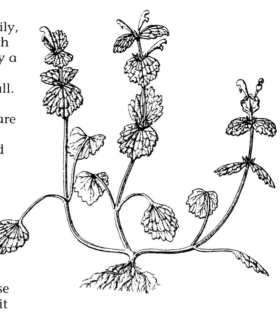

Figure 34. Henbit (*Lamium amplexicaule*).

Ground Ivy
(*Glechoma microcarpa*)

Other Names: Creeping Charlie

Life Span: Cool season perennial

Description: Ground ivy is a member of the mint family which was originally introduced as a ground cover. Ground ivy thrives under shaded conditions, but can be found in direct sun as well. Ground ivy spreads rapidly by creeping stems which are four-sided, square, and capable of rooting at the nodes. The leaves which rise on petioles from the stems are rounded, toothed, deeply veined, and are opposite. The flowers are tubular or trumpet-shaped, lavender in color, and arise from the leaf axils. Ground ivy flowers in the early spring.

Figure 35. Ground ivy (*Glechoma microcarpa*).

Prostrate Spurge
(*Euphorbia supina*)
Spotted Spurge
(*Euphorbia maculata*)

Other Names: None

Life Span: Warm season annual

Description: Prostrate spurge and spotted spurge are similar in appearance. All plant parts contain a white, milky sap. The stems radiate from a taproot, forming a dense mat, especially in the case of prostrate spurge. Spotted spurge has smooth stems, while prostrate spurge has hairy stems. Leaves are opposite, oblong, and may have a reddish splotch in the center. The leaves of spotted spurge are somewhat toothed, while prostrate spurge has smooth leaves with some hairs on the underside. Small, inconspicuous flowers are produced in the upper leaf axils. Prostrate and spotted spurge germinate in late spring and bloom into September. They are usually a problem in thin, stressed turfs.

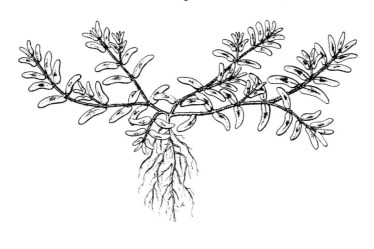

Figure 36. Prostrate spurge
(*Euphorbia supina*).

Prostrate Knotweed
(*Polygonum aviculare*)

Other Names: Knotweed

Life Span: Cool season annual

Description: Prostrate knotweed is a low growing annual which is typically found in compacted soil. It is one of the first plants to emerge each spring, with germination occurring in March. The stems, which radiate from a central taproot, are tough, slender, wiry, and produce mat-like growth. Leaves rise from the nodes which are surrounded by a thin, papery sheath. The leaves are dull green, alternate, oblong, and pointed at the tip. Flowers are small, inconspicuous, and in clusters in the leaf axils.

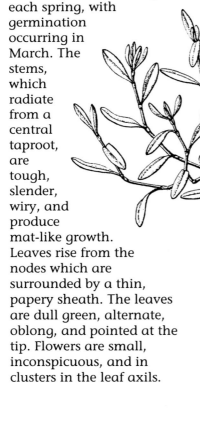

Figure 37.
(*Polygonum aviculare*).

Dandelion (*Taraxacum officinale*)

Other Names: None

Life Span: Cool season perennial

Description: Dandelion is probably the most widely recognized turfgrass weed. Dandelion is a simple perennial, having a thick, fleshy taproot which can penetrate into the soil 2 feet or more. The above ground portion consists of a rosette of basal leaves. The leaves are long, deeply notched, with the lobes pointing back toward the crown. Flower stalks rise from the crown area and are long, hollow, and hairy. Both the leaves and the flower stalk contain a white, milky sap. The flowers produced on the stalks are bright yellow round clusters, but turn into a white puff-ball full of seeds upon maturing. The seeds are attached to a long, parachute-like pappus, capable of carrying the seed great distances. It is one of the first plants to emerge each spring, but seedlings can occur throughout the growing season.

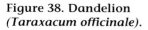

Figure 38. Dandelion (*Taraxacum officinale*).

Purslane (*Portulaca oleracea*)
Other Names: None
Life Span: Summer annual
Description: In new seedings or thin turf, purslane can become a very troublesome annual. Like many desert plants, it has the ability to store moisture for great lengths of time. It thrives in extremely hot, dry weather. The sprawling stems of purslane are thick, round, fleshy, and reddish-brown in color. Leaves are bright, shiny-green, wedge-shaped, rubbery, and thick. Purslane has tiny yellow flowers with five petals. These flowers seldom open unless the sun is shining brightly. The cup-shaped seedpods produce an abundance of small, black seeds. These seeds may lie dormant in the soil for many years.

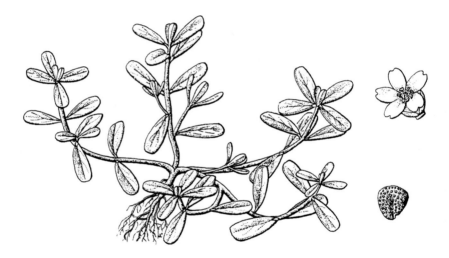

Figure 39. Purslane (*Portulaca oleracea*).

Blackseed Plantain
(*Plantago rugelii*)
Broadleaf Plantain
(*Plantago major*)

Other Names: None

Life Span: Cool season perennial

Description: Blackseed and broadleaf plantain are similar in appearance. The plantains are simple perennials, having a mostly shallow, fibrous root system. The above ground portion consists of a rosette of basal leaves. The leaves are large, oval to elliptic, with conspicuous veins, and have a long petiole attached to the crown. Blackseed plantain has purple coloration at the petiole base, while the petiole of broadleaf plantain is green and somewhat shorter. Long, rat-tail like flower stalks extend up to 12 inches and produce numerous, inconspicuous flowers.

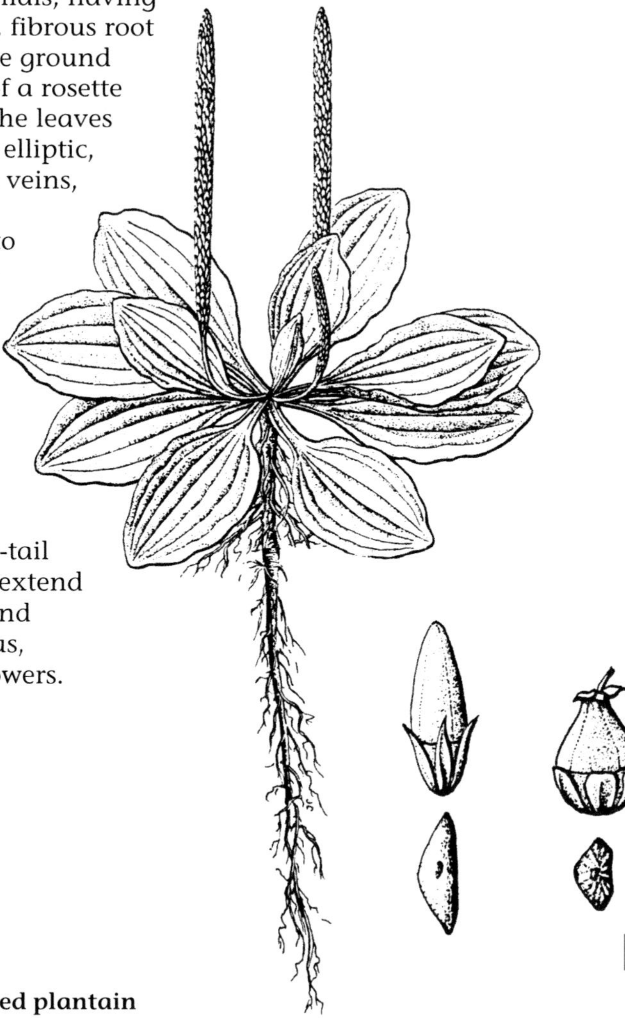

111

Figure 40. Blackseed plantain
(*Plantago rueglii*).

Violets (*Viola spp.*)

Other Names: None

Life Span: Cool season perennial

Description: Violets are one of the first plants to flower in the spring and are usually found in shaded, moist areas. The violets have a dense, fibrous root system. The above ground portion is stemless, with heart-shaped basal leaves. The leaves are scalloped on the edge and attached to the crown by long petioles with prominent stipules. The flowers are borne on long stalks and are light blue to deep purple in color.

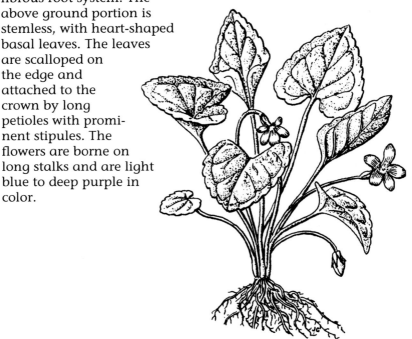

Figure 41. Violet (*Viola spp.*).

Field Bindweed
(*Convolvulus arvensis*)

Other Names: Creeping Jenny

Life Span: Warm season perennial

Description: Field bindweed usually invades thin, drought-stressed turf. The plant grows prostrate, close to the soil surface and is able to tolerate close mowing. The slender stems can grow several feet long and can climb short distances. The leaves are alternate, petioled, and are generally spade-shaped with pointed, basal lobes. The size and shape of the leaves vary, depending on environmental conditions. Field bindweed reproduces from seed and an extensive root system. The flowers are conspicuous, trumpet-shaped, and white or pink. Roots may extend 20 feet into the soil.

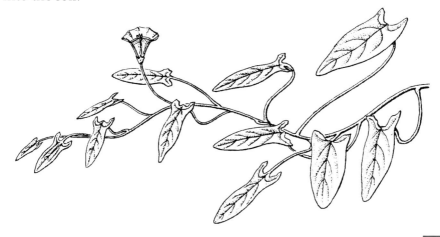

Figure 42. Field bindweed
(*Convolvulus arvensis*).

Speedwell (*Veronica spp.*)
Other Names: None
Life Span: Winter annual
Description: The speedwells are low growing initially, then grow erect at maturity. The stems are hairy and branched. The leaf shape varies, but typically leaves are small, hairy, and opposite. The lower leaves are round to oval and bluntly toothed. The upper leaves are lance-shaped and narrow. Flowers are small and blue with white throats. The distinctive seedpods are two-celled and heart-shaped.

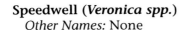

114

Figure 43. Speedwell (*Veronica spp.*).

Common Mallow (*Malva neglecta*)

Other Names: Cheese Weed

Life Span: Cool season annual/biennial

Description: Common mallow produces a deep, white, fleshy taproot and sends out trailing branches. The leaves, which are borne on long petioles, are large, alternate, hairy, and round with toothed margins. Flowers are small, with five petals, and white to lilac in color.

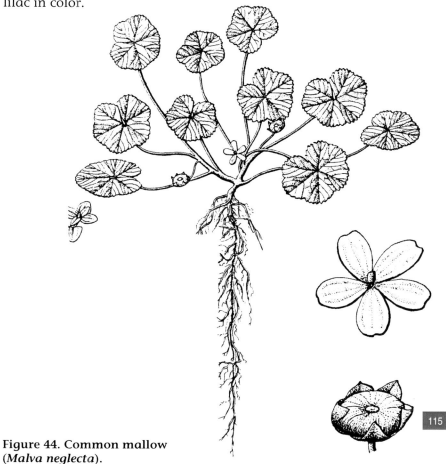

Figure 44. Common mallow (*Malva neglecta*).

Moss and Algae

Moss and algae are green plants, which requires their discussion as a turf pest in this chapter. Moss and algae infestations in turf are indicative of poor drainage or air circulation, dense shade or waterlogged soils. Both organisms thrive under excessively fertilized or irrigated turf. Moss is a light green, low-growing collection of plants which feel velvety when touched. Moss is normally found growing on bare soil in shaded turf areas. Algae appears as a green to black, slimy scum that covers both bare soil and thin turf areas. Control methods range from aggressive raking to chemical applications. These approaches, however, are short-term at best. For permanent eradication of mosses and algae, identify and eliminate the conditions which are favoring their growth.

Weed Management

The best defense against weeds is a thick, well-managed turf. A vigorous turf will successfully compete with weeds for light, nutrients, and water. Weeds become established most readily in thin, weak stands of turf. Spraying weeds by itself does not usually produce satisfactory,

long-term results. Although herbicides can be used in an integrated weed control system, proper management can do much to encourage a dense, vigorous turf and discourage weeds. Refer to Chapter 1, *Integrated Turfgrass Management*, for a review of proper turfgrass management.

Herbicides are available to control most turf weeds. Care should be used when applying any pesticide. Always read and follow label directions. Improper use can result in poor weed control, turf injury, or injury to sensitive ornamental or garden plants.

Preemergence herbicides are applied to the turf before weeds germinate. They are used primarily to control annual grasses such as crabgrass, but also may control certain annual broadleaf weeds. These products should be applied several weeks before weeds germinate. To control most annual grasses, apply preemergence herbicides when soil temperature exceeds 50°F. A second application is sometimes needed to provide season-long control. Preemergence herbicides should be watered in immediately after application with at least 1/2 inch of water.

Postemergence herbicides are sprayed once the weed has emerged and are applied to the foliage of actively growing weeds. Most postemergence herbicides control broadleaf weeds, and some are available for grasses.

There are several factors which influence the effectiveness of postemergence herbicide applications. Control is easiest to achieve when the weeds are small, healthy, and actively growing. As the weeds age, changes in the leaf surface, growth habit, and physiological function occur. These changes result in reduced herbicide uptake and translocation.

Avoid mowing for several days before and after postemergence herbicide application. Mowing before application reduces the amount of weed foliage available to intercept the chemical and causes stress which reduces herbicide uptake. Mowing after application may remove the treated portion and prevent translocation to the roots.

Do not apply postemergence herbicides to turfgrass and weeds under heat or drought stress. Injury may occur to the turfgrass and weed control can be less effective. Water the turf thoroughly before application to assure that the weeds are actively growing. Unlike the preemergence herbicides, don't water for several days after application. Watering can wash the herbicide off the plant. Also, avoid spraying if rain is expected within 24 hours.

Many postemergence herbicides for the control of broadleaf weeds are very volatile, and may injure sensitive plants in the area. Care should be taken to only spray when the wind is 5 mph or less, and the air temperature is less than 80°F. Postemergence broadleaf herbicides are either applied early in the spring (April-May) or in the fall prior to the first frost.

Herbicides are a useful tool for controlling weeds, but they only provide short-term relief. The best approach is to use an integrated system which utilizes proper mowing, fertilizing, and irrigation management to establish a vigorous turf.

Diseases of Cool Season Turfgrass in the Great Plains

John E. Watkins
Extension Plant Pathologist

- Leaf spot and melting out
- Red thread
- Dollar spot
- Necrotic ring spot and summer patch
- Brown patch
- Pythium blight
- Powdery mildew
- Rust
- Stripe smut
- Ascochyta leaf blight
- Septoria leaf spot
- Fairy ring
- Slime molds
- Snow molds
- Less common diseases

T urfgrass diseases result from the complex interaction of pathogen, host, and environment. Turfgrass management practices can affect all three, greatly influencing disease development. The interaction of management, environment, and disease is not fully understood. Those practices that favor vigorous, but not lush, grass growth and are detrimental to growth of the pathogen result in less disease injury. Good turfgrass management is an effective disease deterrent.

Leaf Spot and Melting Out

Leaf spot and melting out are two fungal diseases of turfgrass within the "Helminthosporium" leaf, crown, and root disease complex. The leaf spot pathogen, *Bipolaris sorokiniana*, attacks bluegrasses, bentgrasses, ryegrasses, and fescues. Melting out, caused by *Drechslera poae*, is the most serious disease of Kentucky bluegrass and also occurs on ryegrasses and fescues. *B. sorokiniana* is a warm weather pathogen and *D.*

poae is a cool weather pathogen.

Both diseases are favored by dry periods alternating with prolonged cloudy, wet weather. Leaf spot is most active at temperatures between 70°F and 85°F. Optimum temperatures for melting out are 65°F to 75°F. Under these conditions, both pathogens produce tremendous numbers of spores on plant debris. These spores are spread to new growth by wind, mowers and other turf equipment, splashing water, foot traffic, dragging hoses, and infected grass clippings. The spores germinate when they contact water droplets on the leaf. The fungus can enter the leaf within hours. Symptoms appear and a new crop of spores can be produced within 7 to 10 days.

Leaf spot.

Melting out.

Leaf spot in bentgrass.

spots with buff-colored centers surrounded by a dark-brown to dark-purple margin. Melting out starts out as black to purple spots on the leaf blades and sheaths. Infected leaf sheaths turn a uniform dark, chocolate brown, causing leaves to yellow and then drop from the plant. From a distance, affected turf appears yellow and thin.

Symptoms on bentgrasses differ from those on the other hosts. Infection of bentgrass golf greens gives a smokey blue cast to the turf that progresses to a yellowing and finally complete blighting of the leaves and thinning of the turf. The affected area conforms to a definite pattern with distinct margins.

Leaves within the affected area are water-soaked and matted. On bentgrass fairways initial symptoms are yellow flecks on the leaves that develop into small oval lesions and then into irregular water-soaked blotches.

A variety of leaf spot symptoms accompany the stages of disease development. Early symptoms are small, dark-purple to black spots on the leaf blade. Older symptoms are round to oval

The most effective preventive for leaf spot and melting out combines the use of improved cultivars with good turfgrass management practices and fungicide sprays. Only improved disease resistant cultivars should be used for new turf establishment or turf renovation. Good cultural practices include a fertilization program that does not stimulate lush growth, thatch management, watering in the early morning, and a mowing frequency adjusted to the growth of the grass. When necessary, apply a fungicide beginning in April followed by two or three additional applications spaced three to four weeks apart.

Red Thread

The key components to outbreaks of red thread, caused by the fungus *Laetisaria fuciformis*, are cool moist conditions coupled with slow grass growth. It is especially damaging to turf whose growth has been slowed because of low temperatures or low fertility. Red thread has become a serious problem on golf greens and fairways with the recent trend toward lower nitrogen rates

on bentgrass. The application of growth regulators that retard plant growth also may increase the incidence of red thread. Weakened turf will continue to decline until corrective measures are taken to control the disease.

Drizzly days with temperatures between 65°F and 75°F are most conducive to the development of red thread. Disease activity ceases during hot, dry weather but may resume in the fall. *L. fuciformis* survives the summer and winter as sclerotia and dormant mycelium in infected host tissue. The disease is spread by equipment contaminated with the causal fungus. Mowing turf in early morning when it is wet with dew contributes to the spread. Fungal structures also can be spread by wind or carried by

Red thread.

Dollar spot lesion.

running water. Individual diseased patches enlarge as the pathogen grows from leaf to leaf. When moisture droplets collect on the leaves, the fungal mycelium penetrates through the leaf stomates and cut leaf tips. Leaf death can occur within two days after infection.

Symptom patterns are circular to irregular patches with a pinkish to tan cast. The presence of uninfected leaves intermingled with infected leaves gives the patch a scorched or ragged appearance, and from a distance the turf may appear to be suffering from drought. Infected leaves die from the tip downward, but infection is confined to leaves and leaf sheaths. During wet weather, affected leaves may become covered with pink gelatinous flocks of

mycelium that sometimes bind the leaves together. When wet the patches not only appear pink but feel slimy to the touch. Pink to coral, threadlike fungal structures (sclerotia) protrude from the tips of infected leaves as branched, antlerlike appendages (red threads). The presence of these appendages distinguishes red thread from pink patch. They can be seen without the aid of magnification.

Maintaining an adequate and balanced fertility program can help prevent severe infection. When the disease is active, collect grass clippings. On turf with a history of red thread, start a preventive fungicide program when day temperatures are 60°F to 70°F. Treatments should be repeated every 10 to 14 days as long as wet weather persists. For a curative program treat the turf every four to five days until it recovers.

Dollar Spot

The presence of dollar spot in a well-managed turf affects its aesthetics or recreational use, but is usually not a threat to its survival. Dollar spot is caused by the fungus *Sclerotinia homeocarpa*.

Warm days and cool nights that produce dew and high humidity in the turf canopy are ideal conditions for dollar spot. Under these conditions, the dollar spot fungi produce mycelium on the surface of grass blades, which is spread with the clippings, mowers, and foot traffic. Dollar spot can appear any time from late spring through late autumn and may become severe in turf deficient in nitrogen.

Overall disease appearance on closely mowed bentgrass golf greens are round, light tan ranging from the size of a quarter to a silver dollar. On turfs maintained at 1 to 3 inches, symptoms appear in a mottled, light tan pattern made up of 4- to 6-inch patches of blighted turf. Individual leaf blades will develop a lesion that may be up to an inch long, is light tan with reddish-brown margins, and usually spans the

width of the blade. When dew is present, the mycelial growth on the grass blades looks like a cobweb.

Dollar spot often can be prevented without the use of fungicides or with minimal fungicide application. Proper

Dollar spot in Kentucky bluegrass.

Dollar spot mycelium.

fertilization to ensure vigorous, but not overly lush growth, morning watering, reducing thatch and compaction, and early morning syringing to reduce dew are usually sufficient to prevent damaging outbreaks. If needed, a fungicide can be applied at the first appearance of dollar spot.

Necrotic Ring Spot and Summer Patch

Two of the most destructive patch diseases of turfgrass are necrotic ring spot, caused by *Leptosphaeria korrae*, and summer patch, caused by *Magnaporthe poae*. Necrotic ring spot generally occurs on Kentucky bluegrass during spring and fall, and summer patch during the hot portion of the summer.

Necrotic ring spot most commonly occurs when wet weather is followed by hot, dry periods. Kentucky bluegrass is the primary host, but the disease can occur on red fescue and *Poa annua*. Summer patch is most active in turfs irrigated by frequent rain or watering. It is common in most turfs, but certain environmental, site, or cultural conditions will enhance development of symptoms. These conditions include heavy thatch, low mowing in midsummer, unbalanced fertility, compaction, a site with a steep slope or which is exposed to heat, and poorly adapted grasses.

Symptoms of these diseases are virtually indistinguishable in affected turf areas, making laboratory examination necessary. Laboratory identification takes three to six months and is not a simple procedure. Affected turfs show 6- to 12-inch circular, semi-circular, or serpentine patches giving the area a pockmarked or doughnut appearance. The dead grass is light tan and matted, and many of the patches will have a tuft of apparently healthy grass in the center. This is often referred to as the "frog-eye" symptom. Plants at

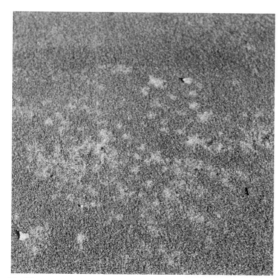

Dollar spot in bentgrass.

the edges of the patches may be unthrifty due to a rotting of the roots by either of the pathogens. If symptoms occur in midsummer, the disease is probably summer patch; but if they show up in spring or fall, the disease is more likely necrotic ring spot.

On established turfs, the most important control is to eliminate plant stresses that favor disease development. The key to prevention is to avoid management practices that promote rapid top growth at the expense of root development. Reducing thatch, growing improved and disease-resistant cultivars, fertilizing and watering properly, syringing heat exposed turf during midday in July and August, eliminating compaction, and using proper mowing height and frequency are cultural practices that will prevent serious injury from either disease. On turfs with a history of necrotic ring spot

or summer patch, fungicides will effectively control the two diseases when applied from mid April to early June with one or two additional applications at three- to four-week intervals.

Necrotic ring spot.

Summer patch.

Brown Patch

Brown patch, caused by *Rhizoctonia solani*, occurs on all commonly cultivated turfgrasses. Kentucky bluegrass, tall fescue, and perennial ryegrass can be seriously injured in midsummer by brown patch. The brown patch pathogen enters the leaf through natural openings and the cut ends of leaf blades.

The disease is common on dense, heavily fertilized and watered turf in hot, humid weather. Often a midsummer fertilization will induce an outbreak of brown patch. High levels of nitrogen and low levels of phosphorus or potassium and nightly irrigation contribute to increased disease severity.

On home lawns, golf course fairways, and other turfs, two general types of symptoms can appear either simultaneously or separately. Field expression of the disease is the presence of patches or rings of dead and dying grass. These patches may be up to 2 feet in diameter, and the grass within these patches may either be matted or standing. Green plants within the diseased patches

Brown patch in bluegrass.

Brown patch in a bentgrass green.

have leaf spots that are long, irregularly shaped, ash-gray areas surrounded by a dark-brown margin.

Preventive measures include summer fertilizing and watering practices that do not stimulate lush growth or keep the turf wet for six to eight hours. Turfgrass cultivars with greater resistance to brown patch should be grown where possible. Controlling thatch and other standard turf management practices also help reduce brown patch injury. On home lawns, fungicide treatment can be started at the first appearance of symptoms. However, for golf courses a preventive fungicide program beginning in June and continuing into mid August is advised. A curative fungicide program can be used on courses where budgets for fungicides are limited. Apply a fungicide at the curative rate when brown patch is first detected.

Pythium Blight

Pythium blight, sometimes called "grease spot" or "cottony blight," is no longer only a disease of golf courses; it is becoming a problem in home lawns and other turfs. Pythium blight is caused by several species of *Pythium fungi*; however, the two most commonly associated with the disease are *Pythium aphanidermatum* and *P. graminicola*. These fungi are in a group known as "water molds" because they grow best under wet, saturated soil conditions. In turfgrass they survive in thatch and soil. All turfgrass species are susceptible to attack by Pythium blight fungi.

The two most important criteria for disease occurrence are poor soil drainage and a wet turfgrass canopy. Water-logged soils and a moist thatch layer, along with high relative humidity and day temperatures above 90°F with warm nights, provide an ideal environment for an outbreak

Brown patch in tall fescue.

of Pythium blight. The *Pythium* is spread when infected grass blades cling to shoes, mowers and other equipment, and when the fungus is moved by flowing surface water.

Early symptoms of Pythium blight are small, roughly circular, reddish-brown spots that suddenly appear in the turf. The pattern of symptoms may develop into streaks that conform to surface drainage channels, remain as random diseased spots, or form into larger areas where the individual spots have merged. The onset of symptoms is rapid during hot, humid conditions. When dew is present, infected leaves are characteristically water-soaked, slimy to the touch, and may contain a mass of fungal mycelium resembling a fluffy cotton ball. Sometimes the infected area will give off a fishy odor. Pythium blight is most easily diagnosed in the early morning when the cottony mycelium is present.

Pythium blight in a bentgrass green.

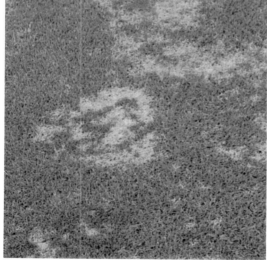

Pythium blight in a ryegrass fairway.

No single control measure will provide complete protection against an outbreak of Pythium blight. Turf managers must employ a combination of good management, early

129

disease detection, and preventive fungicide applications to avoid injury. Management techniques include providing good surface and subsurface drainage, fertilizing in a manner that does not stimulate lush growth, thinning adjacent landscape plantings to promote air movement over the turf, and avoiding trafficking wet turf. Turf with a history of Pythium blight should be treated with a fungicide when humidity is high and day time temperatures are above 90°F and night time temperatures are above 70°F.

Powdery Mildew

Powdery mildew occurs on a variety of cultivated cool-season grasses. It is a common problem on Kentucky bluegrass and fine-leaved fescue turfs in shady areas. Powdery mildew is caused by the fungus *Erysiphe graminis*. This highly specialized fungus may attack only certain cultivars of

one or a few turfgrass species. Mildew chiefly occurs in spring, late summer, and autumn.

Powdery mildew develops in areas of dense shade where air movement is poor.

Pythium blight in ryegrass.

Pythium blight mycelium.

Moderate temperatures, high humidity, and cloudy weather favor outbreaks of mildew. Turf areas under large shade trees and along the north and east sides of buildings are particularly vulnerable to mildew.

The mildew fungus attacks the surface of grass leaves where it produces a white to light-gray powdery growth. Infected leaves become yellowed and later turn tan or brown. Turf in heavy shade looks as if it had been dusted with lime. Turf composed of susceptible cultivars or newly seeded turf can be thinned by severe infection.

Mildew can be controlled by selective pruning of shade trees to increase light penetration and improve air movement that dries the grass canopy. Resistant cultivars of Kentucky bluegrass and fine-leaved fescues should be used in shaded areas. Fungicides can be used to treat high value turf or turf with a persistent mildew problem. One or two applications in spring, late summer, or autumn provides effective protection against turf loss from mildew.

Rust

Rust diseases, caused primarily by *Puccinia spp.*, occur on all commonly grown turfgrasses. Like the mildews and smuts, rust fungi are highly specialized as to host preference. Two of the more common turfgrass rusts are *P. graminis*, causing stem rust on Kentucky bluegrass, and

Powdery mildew.

P. coronata, causing crown rust on ryegrass and tall fescue. The severity of rust outbreaks varies from year to year. Kentucky bluegrass, perennial ryegrass, tall fes-cue, and zoysiagrass are the turfs most affected by rust.

Rust usually occurs from mid to late summer until early October following hot, dry periods when grass growth has slowed. It becomes severe when lack of water, low fertility, or soil compaction reduce turf growth. Warm days and moderate night temperatures along with long dew periods or night watering create optimal environmental conditions for rust. For infection to occur, the turf must remain wet continu-ously for six to eight hours. In mild winters or in mild climates, rust can survive in infected plants. However, in the central and northern Plains most of the rust overwinters in the south and spores are carried north by winds during the growing season. Variable survival of the fungus is one reason for the sporadic nature of the disease and the late season buildup of rust.

Heavily rusted turfs appear yellow or orange when seen from a distance. Clouds of orange rust spores quickly discolor shoes, mowers, grass catchers, and pant legs. Close examination of rusted leaf

Stem rust in Kentucky bluegrass.

Heavily rusted turf.

blades reveals the presence of orange to brick-red pustules. Spores within these pustules rub off easily when touched. Each rust pustule produces a vast number of spores, each of which is capable of infecting a grass blade. New infections occur about every seven to ten days. Under ideal conditions, turf can become heavily rusted about 40 days after initial infection. Heavily rusted turfs are weak and thin, making them more susceptible to winter injury and other environmental stresses.

Rust management begins with the use of improved rust-resistant turfgrass cultivars. Maintaining the turf in a vigorous but not lush condition by proper fertilization, early morning watering, and aerating to alleviate compac-

tion are recommended to prevent injury from rust. Regular mowing also reduces the risk of severe rusting in late summer and autumn. Fungicides may be needed to control rust on sod fields and on other turfs in certain years with the initial application in early July followed by one or two additional treatments at three-week intervals. However, under most situations good management will be sufficient to prevent severe rusting in late summer.

Stripe Smut

Smut fungi infect a wide variety of grasses, both wild and cultivated. In turfgrass one of the most common smut diseases is stripe smut, caused by *Ustilago striiformis*. Stripe smut is a cool weather disease that shows up in spring and sometimes in autumn. Unlike some smut fungi which are highly host specific, the stripe smut fungus infects most turfgrasses grown.

Stripe smut predominates in midspring when temperatures are in the 50°F to 65°F range. Disease activity ceases during hot weather but may resume in autumn. Once a plant is infected it

Stripe smut close up.

remains infected for life. Smut spores can remain dormant in the thatch for up to three years and are spread by traffic, wind, rain, and irrigation during turf maintenance.

Stripe smut causes grass plants to exhibit a general decline including stunted growth, yellowing, and early death. Smutted plants usually occur in 6- to 12-inch circular patches which are very noticeable in spring due to their light-green or yellow color. At first, leaves on infected plants show yellow stripes that turn gray then black. In time, infected leaves shred and curl. The rupturing of the smutted leaves releases masses of spores into the thatch. Infected plants usually die during hot weather causing the turf to appear thin in affected areas.

Cultural practices have only a limited influence on smut infection and development and are not that useful as control measures. Fortunately, many turfgrass cultivars are resistant to stripe smut. Using resistant cultivars and early morning watering will reduce the risk of turf loss to the disease. Systemic fungicides are effective and should

Stripe smut.

Ascochyta blight in Kentucky bluegrass.

be applied once or twice in April and again in October.

Ascochyta Leaf Blight

Ascochyta leaf blight is a common but minor turfgrass disease. Kentucky bluegrass, perennial ryegrass, tall and red fescues, and bentgrasses can be attacked by one of several species of the fungus *Ascochyta*.

Periods of wet weather or frequent watering favor the disease during late spring and summer. *Ascochyta* survives in the thatch and infects grass leaves during periods of rain. The fungus enters through freshly cut leaf ends and grows toward the base of the leaf. Frequent mowing, particularly with a dull mower, increases infection.

Ascochyta blight may cause large areas of turf to be blighted or it may appear only in localized patches. Individual leaves die back from the tip and take on a bleached color. When the disease occurs in localized patches, it somewhat resembles dollar spot except that the individual lesions do not have the reddish-brown margins. When a turf is uniformly infected, it resembles the injury from a dull mower blade.

Injury from Ascochyta blight is seldom extensive so control measures are rarely necessary. No fungicides are registered for use specifically against Ascochyta blight; however, most broad spectrum turfgrass fungicides will provide some protection.

Septoria Leaf Spot

Septoria leaf spot, caused by several species of the fungus *Septoria,* is another minor disease of turfgrass. Most of the cool season turfgrasses can be attacked by *Septoria*.

This disease occurs during cool weather in spring and autumn and rarely produces symptoms during summer. *Septoria* survives the winter and summer months in the

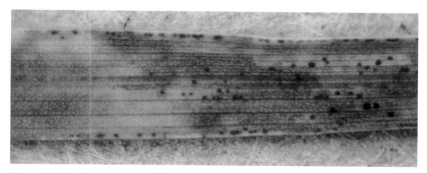

Septoria leaf spot on Kentucky bluegrass.

thatch. During spring rains, spores are splashed or washed onto the leaves where infection usually occurs through freshly cut leaf blades. Repeated infections occur about every 10 days during cool weather.

The overall appearance of a diseased turfgrass area takes on a brown or tan cast and resembles turfgrass injured by a dull mower blade. The leaf blades are light yellow from the tip downward and most have yellow to tan spots near the leaf tip. Close examination shows small black dots called pycnidia, produced by *Septoria*, embedded in the diseased tissue.

No special measures are needed to control this disease.

Fairy ring.

Fairy ring forming mushrooms.

Following the preventive practices outlined for leaf spot and melting out will also provide protection from Septoria leaf spot.

Fairy Ring/Mushrooms

Mushrooms are related to smuts, rusts, and other pathogens, and as such, are members of a large group of organisms called fungi which are devoid of chlorophyll. These fungi are active in the decay of buried stumps and other bits of wood which can contribute to the formation of fairy rings. They appear in clumps or singly; but when they appear in a circular pattern, they are called fairy rings. Although mushrooms are one of nature's ways of recycling nutrients, when they develop in a well manicured turf they are considered a nuisance. No turfs are immune to fairy ring problems. Those with heavy thatch or under stress are more prone to fairy ring development and subsequent turf injury.

The life cycle of fairy ring-forming mushrooms is similar to that of other common mushrooms. Fairy ring fungi survive as dormant spores or mycelium in the thatch and soil. This mycelium becomes active during moderate, wet weather; and the ring continues to grow outward each year. Following rains, mushrooms appear within the dark green ring or at the edge of the dead area. Fairy rings usually are most severe in light-textured, low fertility soils low in moisture. The mushrooms grow on decaying organic matter and are most likely to form in areas where trees have been removed or in turfs with a thick thatch.

Fairy rings are found in three general patterns: (1) mushrooms appear in circles and last only for a brief time, without the presence of a dark green ring; (2) grass growth is stimulated and a dark green ring, along with the presence of mushrooms, is produced; (3) circular patterns of dead grass develop in the center of the dark green ring, along with the presence of mushrooms. The dark green rings of stimulated grass commonly vary from 1 to 10 feet in diameter and are particularly visible on turfs yellowing from iron chlorosis and in midsummer on turf that is deficient in nitrogen or under moisture stress. The dark green grass is caused by a rapid release of nitrogen in the soil. A concentric ring of thin, dormant, or dead grass may develop inside the circle of lush grass as a result of drought stress caused by the dense mat of fungal mycelium present just below the ring.

Tree stumps, large roots, and pieces of construction lumber should be removed before a new turf site is sodded or seeded. In established turfs, symptoms are "masked" by pumping large quantities of water 10 to 24 inches deep into the soil at 1-foot intervals within the ring and at up to 2-foot intervals on either side of it. The procedure should be repeated every two to three weeks during the growing season. A light fertilizer application during the growing season will reduce the contrast in green color between the fairy ring and the rest of the turf. If desired, the fairy ring can be physically removed by carefully digging out the sod to a depth of 12 to 18 inches in a zone 2 feet on either side of the dark green ring of grass and replacing it with fresh topsoil. Another approach is to kill the turf in the infested area with glyphosate and rototill the entire area in different directions to mix the mycelium from the different rings. The area can then be seeded or sodded.

The fungicide flutolanil is registered for the suppression of certain fairy ring fungi. It could be used to spot-treat problem fairy rings in certain areas such as golf greens; however, suppression may be only temporary.

Slime Molds

Slime molds are primitive organisms that exhibit characteristics of both plants and animals, although they are considered fungi. Numerous species of slime mold occur on turf; the most common is *Physarum cinereum*. Slime molds are not pathogens and cause little more than some yellowing.

Slime molds grow on the surface of leaves and stems feeding on decaying organic litter and other fungi and bacteria in the thatch layer and in the soil. They often appear on well-maintained turf after a warm summer rain and usually reappear in the same area year after year and last one to two weeks. Slime mold spores are spread

Slime mold in buffalograss.

by wind, water, mowing, and other activities on the turf.

A slime mold is composed of thousands of tiny, usually purple, gray, white, or cream, sack-like spore enclosures called fruiting bodies. These form in 4- to 6-inch patches in the turf and may be widely spread or clustered into groups. The slimy growth is called a plasmodium. This dries into a powdery mass of spore-bearing bodies that coat the grass blades.

Slime molds are more of a curiosity or nuisance than a threat to the turf. Control measures are usually not necessary; but if desired, slime mold can be removed by vigorous raking, mowing, or hosing down with a fast stream of water.

Snow Molds

Principle snow molds of the central and northern Plains are Microdochium patch (pink snow mold) and Typhula blight (gray snow mold). Other snow molds, such as Sclerotinia patch, also may occur in certain areas.

Microdochium patch, caused by *Microdochium nivale*, can injure turf any time from mid October to April during prolonged cool, wet weather. Infection most often occurs with temperatures between 32°F and 50°F, during cold fogs, or in light drizzle. Conditions that bring on severe damage are heavy, wet snows occurring on unfrozen turf. High nitrogen fertilization in early fall or heavy top dressing will also enhance pink snow mold development.

Symptoms of pink snow mold on bentgrass greens or tees are roughly circular, rusty brown patches that range from 6 inches to several feet in diameter. On Kentucky bluegrass, fine-leaved fescues, and ryegrasses symptoms are more or less circular spots, mostly in the 4- to 12-inch diameter range. Within these spots, the grass is bleached and matted. When wet, a white to

Slime mold fruiting bodies.

salmon-pink moldy growth is visible at the edges of the patches. The scattered spots are easily detected, even in midwinter, because of the contrast in color between the diseased spots and dormant turf.

Unlike Microdochium patch, Typhula blight (gray snow mold) is strictly a cold-weather disease. Typhula blight, caused by *Typhula ishikariensis* or *T. incarnata*, can seriously injure turf during periods of extended snow cover.

The Typhala blight fungi spend the warmer months as sclerotia embedded in infected grass blades and in thatch. Snow cover and near-freezing temperatures trigger germination of sclerotia and infection of grass plants. Early winter snows that are wet and

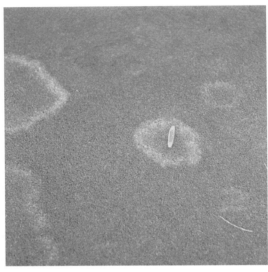

Microdochium patch on bentgrass.

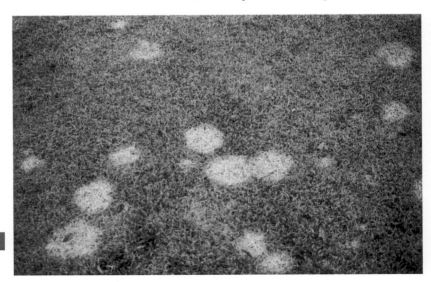

Microdochium patch on Kentucky bluegrass.

cover the ground for several weeks initiate gray snow mold activity. Turf injury is aggravated when the snow is compacted by walking, skiing, snowmobiling, or sledding.

Symptoms of gray snow mold are most likely to develop where snow has drifted or been piled and is slow to melt. Patches of rough, dead, bleached-tan areas up to a foot in diameter become visible as melting snow recedes from diseased areas. When wet, they are often covered by a whitish-gray moldy growth. *Typhula* develops tiny orange to black sclerotia embedded in infected leaves. They are visible with a hand lens, and a magnifying glass can be used to distinguish between the two snow molds.

Gray snow mold injury to bentgrass.

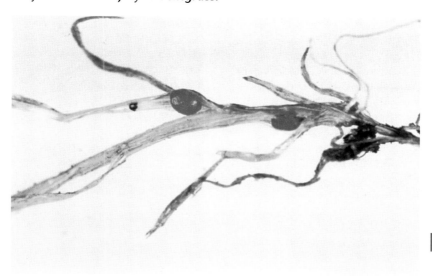

Typhula blight sclerotia.

Snow mold injury can be prevented through management and fungicide application. Dormant fall fertilization with a slow-release nitrogen carrier and mowing until leaf growth has stopped will prevent lush growth going into winter. Use snow fences to prevent drifting on high-value turf and to restrict traffic on frosted or snow-covered turf. Snow mold injury can be repaired by raking the affected turf in early spring and by lightly fertilizing to encourage new growth. Use a preventive fungicide program on high-value turf and on areas where snow molds cause injury year after year. Make the initial application in early to mid November and repeat applications during midwinter thaws, as needed.

Less Common Diseases

Take-All Patch

Take-all patch occasionally injures bentgrass and other turfs in the central and northern plains. It is caused by the fungus *Gaeumannomyces graminis* which attacks the roots of grass plants during cool (50°F to 65°F) wet conditions in spring and fall. The disease produces depressed, circular patches of blight turf. The patches range from 6 inches to 2 feet in diameter and appear bronze to reddish-bronze. The patches may develop the "frog-eye" pattern in which there is a tuft of healthy grass in the center of the patch.

Management practices include maintaining a soil pH below 6.5 and using a balanced fertility program. Applying sulfur, ammonium sulfate, or ammonium chloride in early spring may reduce disease severity.

Rhizoctonia Yellow Patch

Rhizoctonia cerealis causes a disease in annual bluegrass and Kentucky bluegrass called Rhizoctonia yellow patch. This disease is sometimes referred to as "cool weather brown patch". Periods of extended rainfall and 50°F to 65°F temperatures favor this disease. Symptoms are 1 to 3 foot diameter, circular patches in the turf. Leaf blades show a tan discoloration beginning at the tip and progressing downward.

Practices that reduce surface humidity within the turf canopy will restrict disease development. Nitrogen does not appear to directly influence yellow patch; however, a balanced fertility program promotes recovery of injured turf.

Nematode Injury

Nematodes are wormlike aquatic animals that constitute one of the more abundant forms of animal life. Plant pathogenic nematodes that attack turfgrasses live in thin water films on soil particles. About 18 genera of nematodes are known to attack turfgrasses. The role of nematodes as turfgrass pests is not always obvious and often tends to be one of the last things a turf manager or golf course superintendent considers when diagnosing a turf problem that doesn't respond to fertilizer, fungicides, irrigation, or other cultural or chemical practices.

Above ground symptoms produced by root feeding nematodes are a rather nondescript yellowing and thinning of the turf. However, below ground symptoms are more diagnostic of nematode feeding and may appear as stunted root systems, root systems with galls, knots or lesions, or excessively branched root systems.

The decision to apply a nematicide to established turf is based on the damage threshold level. This is the minimum nematode population level per unit of soil (100cc) required for economic damage on a given host and justifies the implementation of control procedures. Not all nematode species are equally damaging at a given population level on a given host. Threshold levels will differ for different nematodes and grass hosts.

To sample for nematodes, use a standard 1-inch soil probe and take a composite sample of 20 cores per 1000 square feet. Make certain that the composite samples are collected from the affected area. It's a good idea to collect a composite sample from a healthy nonaffected area as a basis of comparison. The composite sample volume should be at least one pint. Label the sample and keep it in a cool site until it can be transported to a laboratory for nematode analysis. Proper sampling and interpretation of the results are key factors in the decision to use a nematicide.

On established turf only a limited number of nonfumigant nematicides are available. These should be used with extreme caution and must be watered into the root zone to be effective.

Integrated
Pest Management
of Vertebrates

Scott E. Hygnstrom
Extension Wildlife
Damage Specialist

- IPM overview
- Moles
- Pocket gophers
- Thirteen-lined
  ground squirrels
- Voles
- Skunks
- Canada Geese

Most people thoroughly enjoy viewing wildlife out in the country, in parks, and in their own backyards. The constant activity of songbirds at a feeder or the humorous antics of a squirrel searching for nuts can provide hours of recreational viewing and, perhaps more importantly, a link to our outdoor heritage. Unfortunately, wildlife also can cause backyard problems which may appear to pop up overnight. What was once a spotless lawn can become riddled with mounds of dirt, fresh diggings, or a maze of ridges. Young trees may be nipped or prized flowers clipped. Usually the culprits go unobserved, but the evidence of their activity is quite apparent.

Most vertebrate pest problems in turf are caused by mammals, in particular: moles, pocket gophers, ground squirrels, voles, and skunks.

These animals are usually very shy — in fact, moles and pocket gophers spend their entire lives underground and out of view. Several methods are available to prevent or control their damage; however there are no magic potions. Employing a combination of methods will usually be more effective than relying on a single approach. Before beginning control measures, consider the extent of the problem in relation to control costs. Wildlife can provide many aesthetic, economic, and recreational benefits. Their mere presence does not mean damage will occur.

Moles

The eastern mole, *Scalopus aquaticus (Figure 45)*, is the only mole commonly found in Nebraska. These moles are fairly small animals; as adults, they weigh 3 to 5 ounces and are 4 to 6 inches long. Moles spend most of their lives underground. As a result, few people have ever seen a mole.

The eastern mole is a native species and a natural part of our environment. It plays an important role in soil aeration, mixing, and water infiltration. It has

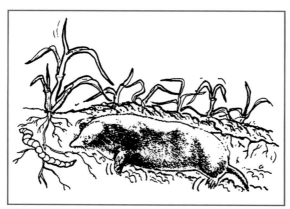

Figure 45. The eastern mole.

very strong forelimbs that are used to burrow through the soil, in a swimming motion, as fast as one foot per minute. Moles usually form permanent burrows and nests 4 to 6 feet underground, beneath trees, fencerows, buildings, or sidewalks. Moles typically live alone, except for a female with her young. Densities rarely exceed three moles per acre.

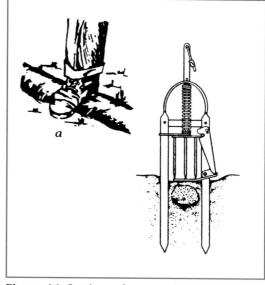

Figure 46. Setting a harpoon trap for moles. Pack down a portion of the surface burrow (a) and push the set trap down over the burrow until the trigger-pan rests firmly on the depressed ridge (b).

Moles have voracious appetites and can eat 70-100 percent of their body weight each day. They feed primarily on insect grubs, adult insects, and earthworms in the soil. Only occasionally do they eat plant materials. When searching for food, moles burrow through the soil, just slightly below the ground surface, pushing up small ridges of turf. They eventually develop an extensive system of ridged feeding tunnels that may wind around in areas up to 100 square feet. Another sign of activity are molehills — small, conical mounds of soil on the surface of the ground.

Most turf damage occurs in the spring and fall when soil temperatures are moderate and moles are actively searching for food just below the surface of the ground. Their tunneling can kill grass and other lawn plants because they damage the root systems. Ridges and molehills also can interfere with mowing.

Prevention and Control

Trapping is the most practical and effective method to control moles. The harpoon-type trap is most commonly used. It is available at many hardware and lawn and garden stores. Choker- and scissors-type traps also are effective. Mole traps are relatively safe for users, pets, and other wildlife.

The best time of year to trap moles is in the spring or fall when they are most active near the soil surface. Set traps over frequently used tunnels, such as those that have fresh signs and run in straight lines. To determine which tunnels are active, flatten sections with your foot and check them a few hours later to see which have been pushed up. Set traps over tunnels that are active and near protective cover (*Figure 46*). Move traps to new locations if they are not successful in two to three days. If a trap is successful, reset it. If it hasn't been sprung again in a day or two, move it to another area.

It is often suggested that if you eliminate grubs from an area you will get rid of moles. Grubs, however, make up only a portion of the mole's diet. During dry periods, moles are known to frequent well irrigated lawns just for moisture. Moles often are present even in grub-free yards. If all the earthworms, grubs, and other soil animals in a lawn are eliminated by repeated insecticide application, moles may be forced to seek other areas. Before moving on, however, moles may increase foraging and burrowing activity for several weeks. Soil insecticides are expensive, will not immediately reduce damage, and are not likely to provide long-term control. In addition, soil insecticides may cause the loss of beneficial soil invertebrates and may be a hazard to songbirds and other desirable wildlife.

Fumigants and toxic baits are registered for use on moles but are not practical in most situations. The gas cartridges available in lawn and garden stores typically do not produce enough gas to effectively fumigate mole burrows. Since moles feed primarily on insects and earthworms, they do not readily accept grain baits or pelletized formulations.

Castor oil and a castor oil product called Mole-Med® have shown favorable results in repelling the eastern mole. In one study, Mole-Med® successfully reduced mole activity in an area for over 30 days. To be effective, the castor oil product must be thoroughly watered into the lawn. Irrigate with 1/2 inch of water, apply the repellent solution, then follow with 1 inch or more of water. Areas that receive extensive irrigation will quickly lose the repellent to leaching. For best results, spray the entire area that is to be protected. Moles will burrow under a perimeter treatment. Homeowners can prepare their own repellent concentrate by mixing 6 ounces of 100 percent unrefined castor oil with

2 tablespoons of liquid detergent in one gallon of water. This mixture, like the commercial product, is diluted at a rate of 1 ounce per gallon of water and applied liberally with a sprayer (covers about 300 square feet of turf). We believe that more rigorous testing should be conducted to determine the effectiveness of this mole repellent.

Several "home remedies" have been used to repel or control moles, such as broken glass, chewing gum, rose thorns, and mechanical windmills. Unfortunately none of these have provided consistent protection. Electro-magnetic, vibrational, or sound-producing devices have been marketed, but their effectiveness has not been proven. They are also very expensive compared to conventional methods. A shrub called "gopher purge" (*Euphorbia* spp.) reportedly has some repellent properties. We do not recommend using this plant, however, because it has not been proven effective and it is an exotic species. In addition, it is poisonous and has been responsible for the deaths of small children.

Pocket Gophers

Two species of pocket gophers inhabit Nebraska — the plains pocket gopher, *Geomys bursarius* (Figure 47), which is common throughout the state, and the northern pocket gopher, *Thomomys talpoides*, which is limited to the northern Panhandle. "Pocket" gophers are so named because of their large fur-lined cheek pouches that are used for carrying food. Adults can weigh up to a pound and are about 1 foot long, including the tail. Like moles, pocket gophers spend most of their lives underground and are seldom seen by humans. These gophers help build soils and add to the biotic diversity of the region.

Figure 47. Plains pocket gopher.

Pocket gophers feed primarily on the roots of various plants and occasionally on stems and leaves. They prefer thick tap-rooted plants over grasses, but they will eat both. When active, pocket gophers leave fan-shaped mounds of soil on the surface of the ground, the result of their underground tunneling (*Figure 48*).

A pocket gopher's tunnel system may extend several hundred feet and result in numerous mounds. Pocket gophers can push up 15 to 20 mounds per day in light, sandy soils. Gopher tunnels generally run 8 to 12 inches below and parallel to the ground surface. Deeper tunnels lead to nests and food storage chambers that may be 5 to 6 feet underground. Pocket gophers generally live alone, except for females with their young. A density of six to eight per acre is considered high.

Most problems occur in the spring and fall when pocket gophers are active near the ground surface. Gopher damage in turf is usually not the direct result of gophers chewing on grass roots. Rather, the mounds are unsightly, smother turfgrass, and

interfere with mowing. Gophers also gnaw into underground wires and irrigation lines, causing considerable damage and expense.

Prevention and Control

Trapping is an effective method for removing pocket gophers in relatively small areas. Several types of gopher traps are available at local hardware stores. Trapping is most effective in the spring and fall when gophers are most active. Locate a fresh mound and probe the ground with a metal rod to find the gopher tunnel beneath the surface. One trap can be set in the lateral tunnel that comes up to the surface, or two traps can be set deeper in the main tunnel (*Figure 49*). If a trap has not been visited in two days, move it. About 10 to 15

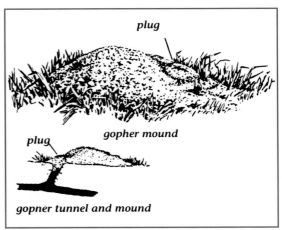

Figure 48. Characteristics of pocket gopher mounds and their relation to a tunnel system.

traps may be needed to efficiently trap one acre.

The use of poison baits is also a cost-effective method for controlling gophers, especially in larger areas. Strychnine is the most widely used toxicant and is commonly formulated as a grain bait with milo, barley, or wheat. Strychnine is labelled as a Restricted Use Pesticide because of its high toxicity and potential hazard to humans and other non-target animals. Other products labeled for pocket gopher control in Nebraska include zinc phosphide, chlorophacinone, and diphacinone. All baits must be placed underground in the gopher tunnel system by using either a hand trowel (*Figure 50*), hand probe, gopher probe, or burrow builder machine. Again, control efforts are most effective in spring and fall. Fumigants and repellents are not effective in reducing pocket gopher damage. Remember to read pesticide product labels thoroughly and comply with all directions.

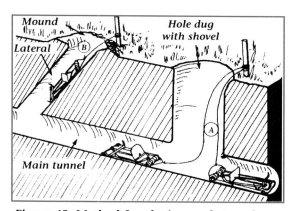

Figure 49. Method for placing pocket gopher traps into a tunnel system.

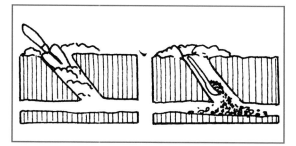

Figure 50. Method for placing pocket gopher bait in a tunnel by hand.

A combination of methods usually will be more effective than relying on any single method. Flooding an occupied area is an effective cultural method of pocket gopher control. Protect buried wires or irrigation lines by either enclosing the wires in or using pipes that are at least 2 1/4 inches in diameter. Gophers cannot open their mouths wide enough to cause damage to pipes of this size. As mentioned in the section on moles, several electronic or magnetic devices are available but their effectiveness is questionable. A plant called "gopher purge" (*Euphorbia* spp.) is sold in many garden catalogues, but is not recommended.

Thirteen-lined Ground Squirrels

Thirteen-lined ground squirrels, *Spermophilus tridecemlineatus* (*Figure 51*) are often referred to as "thirteen liners," "striped gophers," or just simply "gophers." These common names have led to misunderstandings and misapplications of control techniques. Thirteen-lined ground squirrels are fairly small, usually weighing 5 to 9 ounces and measuring 7 to 11 inches long, including the tail. Their most distinctive marking is a set of 13 dark and light stripes and rows of light spots that run the full length of their back. Thirteen-lined ground squirrels are not necessarily gregarious, but densities can average eight to ten per acre in preferred habitat. Unlike many of their relatives, they are active aboveground throughout the day. They are quite bold and in moderate numbers, lend themselves to

frequent and enjoyable wildlife viewing.

During the night and throughout the long winter, thirteen-lined ground squirrels spend their time underground in burrows. Burrows are typically 15-20 feet long and may have two entrances. Entrance holes are usually about 2 inches in diameter and are quite obscure since thirteen-lined ground squirrels do not build mounds. The burrows and subsequent sur-face digging and erosion can disrupt grasses and cause economic damage to turf. Ground squirrels can be particularly troublesome in open grassy areas, such as golf courses, ball parks, cemeteries, and backyards. In addition, they can disrupt gardens and backyard flower beds by excavating seeds and bulbs, clipping young plants, and feeding on ripe fruit and vegetables.

Figure 51. Thirteen-lined ground squirrel.

Prevention and Control

Areas can be made less attractive to ground squirrels by allowing grasses to grow tall and dense. This approach is only suitable where it is compatible with neighboring land-use practices. Reducing or eliminating the mowing of roadside ditches is an effective way to inhibit ground squirrels from invading an area.

In small areas, ground squirrels can be dealt with by trapping. Place a live-trap, made from welded wire, over the burrow entrance (*Figure 52*). Check it several times during the day. To expedite capture, flood the burrow with three to five gallons of water. Release live-trapped ground squirrels in the country in open grassy areas where they will not cause problems for other landowners. Live-traps or rat snap traps also can be set near burrow openings and baited with nuts, seeds, or peanut butter. As a courtesy, notify neighbors of trapping activities.

In larger areas, rodenticides can be used to control ground squirrels. Zinc phosphide is registered for this use and is available in treated-grain bait or pellet formulations. Put one tablespoon of toxic bait directly into each burrow entrance. Toxicants should only be applied below ground to reduce hazards to humans, pets, livestock, and other wildlife species. Read pesticide product labels carefully and comply with all directions.

Since ground squirrel burrows are relatively shallow, fumigants such as aluminum phosphide tablets and gas cartridges can be used effectively to reduce populations to tolerable levels. Place a fumigant directly into the burrow and tightly seal all surrounding burrow openings with soil. Fumigants are most effective when used in the spring. Use care when handling fumigants to avoid setting fires and affecting non-target animals.

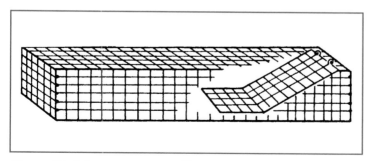

153

Figure 52. A burrow entrance live-trap for thirteen-lined ground squirrels can be made easily with rigid welded wire mesh.

Voles

Voles are small, mouse-like rodents, known to most people as meadow mice or field mice. They are adorable creatures, with large dark eyes, chunky little bodies and velvety fur. We have three species of voles in Nebraska: the meadow vole, *Microtus pennsylvanicus*, prairie vole, *M. ocrogaster*, and pine vole, *M. pinetorum* (*Figure 53*). All weigh only 1 to 2 ounces as adults and measure 4 to 7 inches long, including the tail. They are rarely noticed by humans but are an important part of our environment. Voles typically inhabit roadside ditches, crop fields, woodlots, and other grassy or weedy sites. They can, however, cause problems with lawns and backyard plantings when they overpopulate an area and turn their attention toward tearing up turf and girdling trees and shrubs.

Voles construct surface runways about 1 to 2 inches wide that consist of closely clipped vegetation (*Figure 54*). Small holes in the ground often lead to underground runways and nesting areas. Voles damage lawns by clipping grass close to the roots. Though the damage is usually not permanent, it may detract from the appearance of a well-kept lawn. Voles typically eat leaves, shoots, roots, tubers, and seeds of most grasses and forbs. When food-stressed, especially in winter, voles can cause severe damage to trees and shrubs when they feed on the bark and cause girdling.

Figure 53. The pine vole (top) and prairie vole.

Prevention and Control

Reduce the likelihood of future damage by making the area less desirable to voles. Vole populations cannot grow substantially without food and protection from predators. Control tall grass and weeds in areas adjacent to back-yards, cemeteries, and golf courses. Consider installing 1/4-inch mesh hardware cloth cylinders around trees or shrubs you wish to protect. These cylinders can be time-consuming and expensive to build, but once installed they provide long-term protection from voles and rabbits.

If only a few voles are causing problems, trapping provides good control. Set mouse snap-traps perpendicular to or back-to-back in vole runways, and bait them with peanut butter (*Figure 55*). Multiple-capture live traps also can be very effective because of the gregarious nature of voles. Place traps near recent vole activity and check traps at least twice a day. Release voles in grassy fields or roadside ditches where they will not cause problems for other people.

Rodenticides are more cost-effective in larger areas. Zinc phosphide is registered for vole control and is available in treated-grain bait or pellet formulations. Hand-baiting is the only application method that can be used in urban lawns, ornamental plantings, parks, and golf courses. Place one table-spoon of bait directly into each burrow opening or runway. Use caution when baiting voles to avoid poisoning

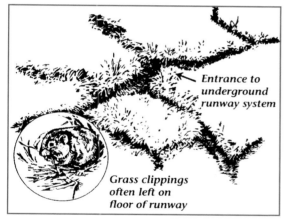

Entrance to underground runway system

Grass clippings often left on floor of runway

Figure 54. The surface runway system of a prairie vole.

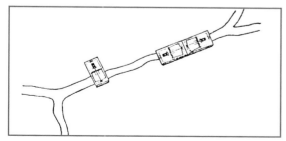

Figure 55. A single trap set in a vole runway, or two traps set back-to-back.

birds and other non-target animals. Read pesticide labels carefully and comply with all directions.

Skunks

Of all the wildlife species that can cause turf problems, perhaps none is quite so unique as the skunk. Of primary concern is their ability to spray a very odorous musk and transmit rabies, a deadly viral disease. In addition, skunks can cause problems in turf, and most people are at a loss as to what can be done about it.

The striped skunk, *Mephitis mephitis* (*Figure 56*) is the only skunk commonly found in the Great Plains. It is black with distinctive white stripes that extend laterally over the back. Adults normally weigh 6 to 8 pounds and are 24 to 30 inches long. Skunks are usually active from early evening through most of the night. During the day they usually sleep in dens under logs, wood piles, or buildings.

Skunks damage turf while searching for food. They eat a variety of plant and animal materials, but prefer insects, such as crickets, grasshoppers, and beetles. They often tear up and destroy turf during their search for white grubs and

other insect larvae. Digging normally appears as 3- to 4-inch cone-shaped holes or patches of overturned sod. This grubbing activity is most common in the spring and fall when larvae are found near the soil surface.

Prevention and Control

Live-trapping and removal is the most common control method for skunks. The offending animals can be caught quite easily in cage traps placed near den entrances or they can be baited into traps using fish-flavored cat food, sardines, peanut butter, or rancid meat (*Figure 57*). Be sure to notify your cat-owning neighbors of your trapping activities. Handle trapped skunks carefully to reduce the risk of being sprayed or exposed to rabies. Cover traps with canvas or a burlap bag before setting and gently slip an old tarp or blanket over the trap when a

Figure 56. Striped skunk.

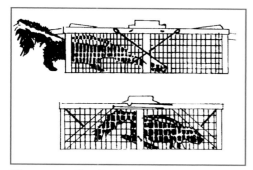

Figure 57. Skunks are easily captured alive in cage traps. Wrap traps with canvas or burlap before setting them.

skunk is captured. Trapped skunks should be transported 10 miles or more in the open box of a pick-up truck and released far away from human dwellings.

For long-term control, consider installing a buried chain-link fence around the perimeter of your property. Also, remove any rockpiles, woodpiles, or other debris that might provide denning habitat for skunks. Soil insecticides can be used to reduce insect populations in turf, thereby making lawns less attractive to skunks. No toxicants are registered for controlling skunks.

Because of the risk of rabies, skunks that show signs of aggressive or abnormal behavior should be destroyed. The Nebraska State Health Department suggests that any skunk that is observed during daylight is acting abnormally and should be destroyed to prevent the spread of rabies.

Such animals are usually shot. Your local law enforcement personnel can provide assistance. Remember that most skunks will release their scent when shot, so try to avoid shooting them near buildings.

Canada Geese

Canada geese, *Brant canadensis (Figure 58)*, have always been a symbol of what is wild and free, but nowadays "goose music" can be heard in busy city parks, golf courses, and even backyards. The draw is water. Goose populations across the continent are approaching all-time highs and many of the birds have taken to inhabiting urban lakes, residential ponds, and even downtown fountains. At first a pair of adults and a gaggle of goslings are a joy for people to watch, but after a few years, two becomes twenty and they begin to wear out their welcome.

Geese readily feed on grass surrounding the ponds and in time can cause significant turf damage. In addition, grass passes through geese quickly and geese often leave their "calling cards" in the most undesirable areas — on golf greens, walkways, and picnic areas. Some city parks and ponds have become so fouled with goose droppings that they are unfit for human use. As if this weren't enough, adult geese actively defend their nests. Unsuspecting youth and adults may be startled, whacked, or chased by geese when they stray too close to a nest.

Geese usually become established in ponds in early spring after returning with their mates from their wintering grounds in the southern United States. A pair will typically establish a territory, build a nest, and raise young by mid-summer. The family will usually fly south in late fall unless food and open water are still available. Some geese have become year round residents as far north as southern Minnesota.

Prevention and Control

Geese can be difficult to disperse once they become established on a pond or feeding site. Begin control measures before the geese become acclimated. Steep-sided ponds are less attractive to geese than ponds with shallow shorelines or open beaches. Overhead grids of wire or monofilament line can be used to keep geese from landing on ponds. Fence geese in or out of areas with 3-foot woven wire fences or short two-strand electric fences.

Turf areas can be made less attractive to geese by selecting the right grass species. Geese prefer bluegrass to tall fescue.

Figure 58. Canada geese.

Therefore, plant tall fescue to reduce grazing in golf courses, parks, or cemeteries. Plant tall trees to interfere with the birds' flight paths and plant shrubs to reduce the birds' on-ground visibility.

A repellent named ReJEX-iT® AG-36 has recently been registered for use on turfgrass. It contains methylanthranilate (grape pop flavoring), a food product that acts as an aversive agent to birds. It has worked quite well in repelling geese from golf course greens and areas around privately owned ponds. Spray a mixture of 2.5 gallons of ReJEX-iT® and 7.5 gallons of water over one acre of turf or two acres of golf green after mowing and allow it to dry. Reapply as needed.

Geese can be frightened from ponds and surrounding turfgrass areas by a variety of visual or noise-making devices. Scarecrows, balloons, flagging, mylar tape, propane cannons, pyrotechnics, sirens, recorded distress calls, and herding dogs have all been used with varying degrees of success. Some general rules are to start early, be persistent, vary your presentation, and use a variety of frightening devices. Be aware that local ordinances may limit your use of some devices such as sirens and cracker shells.

Local flocks of geese that have overpopulated an area can be live captured and transported to other areas if necessary. The adults lose their ability to fly in mid to late June and can be herded into walk-in funnel traps. The goslings that are still unable to fly can be captured at the same time. Federal and state permits are required before geese can be live captured. In addition, a suitable release site must be agreed upon by both federal and state wildlife agencies.

Lethal control may be considered when dealing with Canada geese, but you must abide by federal and state laws affecting such practices. No toxicants are registered for controlling Canada geese or other waterfowl species. The growth of local populations can be slowed by rendering the eggs nonproductive and removing nesting materials. If done correctly, no eggs will hatch and no renesting attempts will occur. Finally, hunting, where safe and legal, is the preferred method of controlling local goose populations. Several cities are now implementing urban hunts to reduce goose numbers. Contact your state wildlife agency for information on goose hunting in your area.

General

Many other species can cause damage to turf, but damage is generally infrequent. While they are usually quite secretive, armadillos, badgers, coyotes, dogs, foxes, and woodchucks have been known to dig up turf in golf courses, cemeteries, and other grassy areas. Cottontail rabbits occasionally scratch out small forms in backyards where they loaf during the day and may hide their young. Raccoons and opossums will tear up turf in search of white grubs, much like skunks do. Even crows and starlings can disrupt turf in their search for soil-borne insects. Contact your local Extension office for information on dealing with such problems.

Remember to use pesticides safely. All fumigants, repellents, and toxicants used to control vertebrate pests can be hazardous to humans, pets, livestock, and non-target wildlife. Only use products registered by the Environmental Protection Agency (EPA) for the intended use. Read pesticide product labels carefully and comply with all directions. Also, be aware of local ordinances and state and federal regulations pertaining to trapping, handling, or shooting problem wildlife.

The book, *Prevention and Control of Wildlife Damage*, provides detailed information on all problem wildlife species in North America. It is available as a two-volume set for $45, CD-ROM for $43, or book/CD-ROM set for $65.

To order make payment by check, money order, or purchase order, payable to the University of Nebraska. Call 402/472-2188 for information or send requests to:

Wildlife Damage Handbook
University of Nebraska
202 Natural Resources Hall
P.O. Box 830819
Lincoln, NE 68583-0819

Abiotic Turf Injury and Disorders

Loren J. Giesler
Plant Pathology
Research Technologist

- Chemical damage
- Water injury
- Drought injury
- Temperature induced injury
- Nutrient deficiencies
- Mowing injury
- Soil-related problems

ellowing or dying patches, parallel striping patterns, or wilting or thinning canopies are often found in problem turf areas. What appears to be the result of an infectious disease or insect damage, often is the result of a chemical application or physical condition in the landscape. Biotic turf problems include disease and insect damage. While non-biotic or "abiotic" problems at first appear biotic, other factors are often responsible for the damage. Examples of abiotic turf injury and disorders include chemical injury due to salt build-up or fertilizer spills; shallow or compacted soils which may be over buried debris; and winter injury resulting from excess ice cover or desiccation of crowns by cold winter winds and a lack of snow cover or top dressing.

Chemical Injury

Management of high quality turf often requires chemical use. Along with the chemical application comes potential applicator errors which result in turf damage.

Pesticides

Any pesticide applied to turfgrass to improve plant health (e.g. fungicides, herbicides, and insecticides) should always be applied in accordance with the product label. Many compounds used for turfgrass disease and pest management have growth regulating properties. Misapplication of pesticides can result in injury or irregular growth of the turf.

Pesticide injury is easily differentiated from disease and insect injury. Generally, the damage will appear in a pattern that corresponds to the method of application and includes broad swaths, narrow streaks, or other regular patterns. Specific symptoms of this type of injury are variable and include chlorosis, leaf speckling, and death, and can

Damage from chemical misapplication.

develop very soon or several weeks after application. Options for correcting the problem include removing the soil, rotating the site into a fallow area, bioremediation, or using activated charcoal to absorb the chemical.

Animal Urine

Dog spot injury.

Urine from animals contains soluble salts, urea, and many other compounds. Often when soluble salt content is high and urine is deposited onto one spot, the turf is killed. The dead area will be surrounded by a margin of dark green, rapidly growing grass. Of all the sources of salts, only animal urine and fertilizer spills result in dead patches with dark green margins. See the *Diagnostic Charts of Common Turfgrass Problems* on pages 179-184 for ways to differentiate this injury from disease and insect damage. Areas of contained damage can be frequently irrigated to remove the salt or salt tolerant cultivars can be planted in known problem areas. In addition,

Dog spot injury.

aeration can enhance drainage. The best overall solution is animal control.

Fertilizers

Excess fertilizer rates usually disrupt the nutrient balances in grass plants. When too much fertilizer is applied, excessive growth is favored which may result in scalping damage during mowing.

163

Green shaded stripes indicative of fertilizer misapplication.

Ice Removal Salt

Salt injury appears as dead or dying patches of turf near roadside areas or sidewalks where salts were applied for snow and ice removal. Symptoms also can occur in patches if snow or ice removal resulted in piling. If dying patches appear in the absence of injury which is diagnostic of disease activity upon careful inspection, and plants cannot be easily pulled from the soil, heavy watering is recommended to dilute the salt concentration before reseeding the area. Areas prone to salt damage (i.e. roadsides and parkways) can

When highly water soluble nitrogen fertilizers, such as urea, are applied to wet turf, salt burn can result. Water turf thoroughly after applying fertilizers to remove any particles from the leaf surfaces and to water in the product. Low application rates associated with misapplication also can cause problems. Turfs often will appear to have green shaded stripes caused by not properly overlapping the fertilizer spreader paths. Always apply fertilizers evenly and at the proper time and rate. Granular applicators should be calibrated regularly to deliver the proper amount of fertilizer.

Roadside salt injury.

be managed by planting salt tolerant cultivars and by removing salt by aerating and watering frequently.

Fuels and Lubricants

Fuel and lubricant spills can severely damage turf, often resulting in long-term damage. One differentiating characteristic of injury from fuel or lubricant spills compared to that of animal urine is the lack of a green margin around the affected area. Hydraulic fluid spills often produce straight line patterns. Most of these chemicals do not include growth beneficial compounds, so turf will often die in the concentrated area of the spill. The spot will have abrupt margins and possibly be irregular in shape. Injury from gasoline, for example, often appears as a roughly circular dead area with a definite margin. Fresh spills can be treated with detergents and then an absorbent, such as activated charcoal, to reduce damage. Acting quickly and containing the spill with absorbent materials will greatly reduce damage. Small damaged areas can be cut out and replaced in high maintenance areas.

Water Injury

The proper balance of water needed for healthy turf is critical; an improper balance of water in a turf ecosystem can result in both biotic and abiotic problems. By knowing how to properly identify these problems, turf managers can minimize damage. In addition, water conservation remains a goal for many turf managers.

Flood or Standing Water

While water is essential to good turf management, too much can create problems. Excess soil water due either to over irrigation or flooding creates

Damage from a chemical spill.

Flooded area (top) and flood damage (bottom).

time and can increase injury.

Turf injury due to flooding appears as dead brown areas. Symptoms will appear a few days after the flood water recedes, and the injured area will follow the outline of low or flooded areas. Depending on the duration of submersion, turf can appear brown but have healthy roots in contrast to root rots. Under long periods of submersion the turf can become partially rotted. As with diagnosis of many turf problems, history of the area is critical to correct identification of the problem. To alleviate the problem, increase surface and soil drainage and select more flood tolerant grasses in problem areas.

Secondary problems associated with excess water are diseases which thrive under extremely moist conditions and take advantage of the stressed plants. One example is Pythium blight which is associated with high canopy humidity and poor drainage.

an unfavorable soil environment for root growth by replacing soil oxygen with water. Without oxygen, root growth is restricted and toxic gases accumulate. This results in plants being weakened and even killed. In addition, standing water in full sun can lead to a condition referred to as scald. Due to the ability of water to resist temperature changes (high specific heat), water temperatures stay warmer for longer periods of

Drought Injury

Drought is defined as prolonged water stress that limits or prevents turf growth. The severity of drought depends on the duration of low water availability. Turfgrass species differ greatly in their ability to withstand drought conditions; this is referred to as drought resistance. Drought injury is related to and often hard to distinguish from high temperature injury.

Symptoms of drought stress begin with the turf taking on a bluish tinge, followed by leaf rolling and, under severe drought, it will eventually turn brown. Drought stressed turf is often found near sidewalks, driveways, or buildings, and at the tops of slopes where increased air movement occurs. Drought stress also can be observed in localized dry spots (hard-to-wet areas) which appear as irregular patterns of dead and dying turf. Causes of localized dry spots include sandy soils, compaction, buried building materials, algal infestations, and fairy rings. Drought stress can be confused with injury caused by subsurface

feeding insects such as billbugs, sod webworms, and white grubs. To differentiate drought from insect injury, examine the turf and determine if insect root feeding has occurred. Curative measures for drought stressed turf and localized dry spots include the use of wetting agents, aerification to improve water penetration and lateral water flow, removal of buried materials, selection of more drought resistant grasses, and deep watering.

A drought related abiotic problem is leaf and crown bruising. During drought conditions, many turfs go into a state of dormancy and their tissues become brittle and are susceptible to bruising. Symptoms of bruising are the entire shoot appearing brown if the crown was damaged or brown streaks on the blades. This can often appear after dormancy is broken and growth resumes

Localized dry spot.

167

Brown striped lawn resulting from leaf and crown bruising by mower wheels.

as brown leaves and shoots which fail to grow. The pattern of injury often is associated with footprints or wheel tracks.

Temperature Induced Injury

Although ambient temperature is a factor of weather patterns, turf canopy temperature is often a factor of management practices. The detrimental effects of temperature depend on the physiology of the turf at the time of a temperature extreme. Fortunately, environmental fluctuations typically occur gradually and allow for an acclimation or adaptation period which allows turf to survive under extreme temperature fluctuations.

High Temperature Injury

High temperatures can result in plant metabolic rate

imbalances. Under normal ambient temperature ranges, plant enzyme systems increase in activity as temperatures increase; however, once temperatures exceed the optimum for growth, enzyme systems shut down. In addition to reducing growth, temperatures above 104° F can break down these proteins (enzymes), causing further plant injury. While ambient temperatures rarely exceed this threshold, turf canopy temperatures can, especially under drought stress. Drought stressed turf canopies can have temperatures 18°F -30°F higher than ambient conditions. In hot summer months, canopy temperatures have been shown to be cooler at higher cutting heights. In addition, by maintaining adequate moisture, canopy transpiration (water loss through the leaf blades) will help maintain a cooler canopy.

High temperature damage can be caused by direct solar radiation, reflected solar radiation from windows or other similar reflective surfaces (increased intensity), objects (containers of hot

Heat injury.

This is the same condition resulting from flooding and high temperatures. Cool season grasses are much more susceptible to high temperature injury than warm season grasses.

To avoid damage, select more heat tolerant grasses and consider syringing turf during hot spells to help keep the turf canopy cooler.

Heat injury.

Low Temperature Injury

liquids, metal pails, car floor mats, storm windows, etc.) placed on turf in full sunlight, and lightning strikes. These heat sources are most detrimental when grasses are not able to cool themselves by evapotranspiration. When turf is covered by any non-permeable material, humidity levels increase and evaporative cooling does not occur. The resulting injury is referred to as scald. Initially turf will appear water soaked, but eventually it will turn brown.

Under specific conditions, extremely low temperatures can damage turf. Generally, low temperature injury results from tissues being mechanically disrupted by internal ice crystals and hydration of the plant crown. This hydration results from the repeated freezing and thawing of the turf. Damage is typically associated with adequate water availability to plant tissue.

Another form of low temperature injury is winter desiccation. Winter desiccation is the result of drying

Winter injury.

Ice-damaged turf.

Tracks from walking on frozen turf.

winds in elevated areas of the landscape. As a protective measure, topdressing and winter blankets can be used on golf greens to avoid low temperature injury. In addition, light watering when air temperatures are above freezing can reduce injury. Selecting grasses adapted to these conditions also would be beneficial.

Frost and Ice Injury

Injury to frosted turf is often associated with traffic from footprints or tire marks, similar to those caused by walking or driving on drought stressed turf. Frozen turfgrass plant tissues become brittle and plant cells are easily damaged by applied pressure.

Irregular areas of damage resulting from ice cracking.

Symptoms of frost injury are straw brown colored turf. Avoid trafficking frosted turf whenever possible.

When ice covers turf for long periods, excess moisture combines with freezing conditions to damage turf. This is often associated with soil compaction. Injury resulting from suffocation of turf due to large sheets of ice often will have discoloration patterns which appear as green irregular strips of turf in the damaged area. They result from ice cracking and oxygen being available at these locations. Ice injury often occurs in pockets or depressions where water can accumulate prior to freezing.

Nutrient Deficiencies

As turfgrasses are cultured for aesthetic reasons, only under extreme nutrient deficiency cases or fertility misapplications (i.e. not overlapping properly) do we actually see symptoms of nutrient deficiency. The typical turfgrass fertilizer contains nitrogen (N), phosphorus (P), and potassium (K). These three nutrients and iron (Fe) are the most common nutrients found to be deficient in turfgrass culture. Deficiencies of each has its own identifiable characteristic.

Nitrogen Deficiency

General yellowing or chlorosis initially in the older leaves is a symptom of nitrogen (N) deficiency. Subsequent to this, tips will die back and shoot density and tillering will decrease. This is the most common nutrient deficiency observed in turfgrasses. Nitrogen deficiency occurs because of the relatively high requirement of nitrogen by most turf species and the inability of most soils to meet this requirement without fertilizer applications. Consult the chapter, *Integrated Turfgrass Management*, for proper nitrogen fertilizer rates for the turf species being managed.

Turf diseases also are affected by nitrogen fertility.

Brown patch may be more active under high levels of nitrogen fertility. In contrast, dollar spot and rust are more active under low levels of nitrogen fertility. By maintaining an adequate nitrogen level, disease management can be enhanced.

Phosphorus Deficiency

A dark green color that progresses to a purplish to reddish purple color, mostly in the older leaves, is a common leaf symptom of phosphorus (P) deficiency. A phosphorus-deficient turf may appear wilted and be confused with one suffering from drought stress.

While leaf symptoms associated with phosphorus deficiency may not be evident, turf performance can be affected greatly. Seedling establishment — the most evident stage at which fertility problems are observed — has been shown to be improved by phosphorus fertility. A high phosphorus fertilizer is recommended for newly seeded areas.

Potassium Deficiency

Yellowing of older leaves followed by tip dieback and necrosis along the leaf margin are signs of potassium (K) deficiency. Typically, symptoms are rare with the exception of sand media greens. Symptoms more likely appear as increased susceptibility to other stresses. Overall turf may appear chlorotic and have lower spring quality and heat resistance. Potassium deficiency is rarely reported, however, it has been suggested that mild deficiencies are rather common. Among various turf species, adequate potassium has been shown to increase establishment and spring performance and to increase stress tolerance to cold, heat, and wear.

Iron Deficiency

Interveinal chlorosis occurring initially in the younger leaves is a sign of iron (Fe) deficiency. In extreme cases, leaves can appear almost white. Iron deficiency results in the loss of an upright growth habit. Turf stands can appear matted and are often difficult to mow. Iron deficient turf may appear as a mosaic of chlorotic patches. Soil conditions leading to iron deficiencies include high soil pH (reduced availability), high soil phosphorus levels (increases plant growth efficiency, i.e. tillering), high soil nitrogen levels (leads to rapid growth rates), sandy soils, and cold, wet soils.

Many products are available for foliar applications of iron. Color enhancement may occur within hours of the application and last two to

Iron (Fe) chlorosis.

Scalping injury.

to unacceptable turf quality. By knowing how to properly identify mower injury and immediately correcting the problem, a healthier turf can be maintained.

Scalping

Removing too much of the turf canopy at one cutting can often result in stress and plant death. Any mowing which removes an excessive amount of top-growth is called scalping. This is typically a problem in unlevel landscapes.

three weeks during wet periods and several months during cool, dry periods. Under high maintenance conditions, iron toxicity can cause a black-ening of leaf tissue, but usually the injury is tempo-rary. Selecting grasses adapted to more alkaline soils also will decrease the problem.

Mowing Injury

The mechanical grazing imposed by mowers is often responsible for injury leading

Symptoms of scalping are brown and yellowing turf associated with closely mowed turf canopies which appear stem-like at elevated areas in the landscape or an area with a hole or depression. The stem appearance results from removing excess vegetation. Damaged areas in rhizoma-tous (lateral root spreading) or stoloniferous (lateral stem spreading) species are normally self-healing. Bunchgrasses, such as tall fescue, may require reseeding.

Dull Blade Injury

Dull mower blades shred the tips of grass blades. Affected blades appear to have small "threads" extending from them. These "threads" are the protruding vascular bundles of the grass blades. Shredding of the tips causes them to turn straw-brown and gives the overall turf canopy a grayish cast.

In addition to decreasing the aesthetic appearance of turf, mower blade injury opens the grass plant up to infection, since the mycelium from certain turfgrass fungal pathogens will enter the leaf through these frayed ends. The best way to relieve these symptoms is to have sharp blades and well maintained mowers.

Dull mower blade injury.

Soil-related Problems

Turf near building sites and high traffic areas may suffer from problems not always obvious to the eye. Shallow soils and compaction result in improper root functioning or root growth being restricted. The end result is increased sensitivity to environmental fluctuations.

Shallow Soils

When soil depth is reduced by some form of rooting inhibitor, the condition is referred to as shallow soils. This condition can result from buried debris or shallow rock outcroppings. Generally turf will not show signs of problems until it is under heat or cold temperature stresses. These areas are more susceptible to environmental conditions (i.e. drought) and become stressed and even die under extreme cases. To resolve the problem, remove the buried debris, if possible,

Damage from compaction.

elevate areas with topsoil, and reseed the area.

Compaction

Soils under turfgrasses in high traffic areas often become compacted to the point of root growth being restricted or improper gas exchange occurring. Water infiltration is reduced and there is a decrease in the porosity which reduces oxygen availability. These areas often conform to foot-paths, animal paths, and areas where heavy equipment follows the same routes. Symptoms of compaction include increased sensitivity to drought, rust diseases, and temperature stresses and appear as browning or low quality turf areas.

Overwatering is a common problem, since compacted soils generally have less air space. Excess water results in slowed root growth and often shallow roots, so when conditions warm up the turf is more easily drought stressed.

Extensive renovations or mechanical aeration can help correct compaction depending on the extent of the problem. Redirect traffic movement from the problem area. Grasses which show increased toler-ance to both wear and compaction also can be selected. The goal of any corrective measure is to improve gas exchange and water and root penetration.

Diagnostic Charts of Common Turfgrass Problems

John C. Fech
Extension Educator for Horticulture
Douglas County

or ease of use, this section has been divided into five charts based on growing conditions. Turfs and pests alike tend to be favored or discouraged by temperature and other weather related factors. Begin diagnosis by considering the current season (i.e. summer) and work through the key, matching conditions in the field to the descriptions under each heading, finally arriving at a possible cause. At this point, turn to other sections of this book to obtain detailed information on the proposed pest or environmental condition suspected to be responsible for the turf decline.

If additional information does not confirm the suspected cause obtained from the key, go back to the field and take another sample or examine factors previously not considered. Complete the diagnosis with another trip through the key, armed with additional observations.

When making observations of a particular problem area, don't overlook previous weather, traffic, and usage factors which may have impacted turf appearance. Current conditions are usually the ones to consider first, however, in many cases, weather or other previous activities on the turf (spills, traffic, etc.) are responsible.

Accurate Application and Placement of Chemicals on Turfgrass

Robert D. Grisso
Extension Engineer

- Liquid applicators
- Sprayer nozzles
- Technology to improve accuracy
- Granular application equipment
- Sprayer calibration
- Tank mixing pesticides
- Granular equipment calibration
- Looking ahead

esticides and fertilizers used in landscape management are normally applied as a liquid through spray equipment or as a granular formulation through dry application equipment. Each method and type of equipment has advantages and disadvantages. Selecting the right application equipment depends on economics, availability, and suitability for the intended use.

Liquid Application Equipment

Over 75 percent of all pesticide applications are made as liquid sprays. Spray equipment ranges from simple hand-operated, non-powered applicators to complex multi-nozzle, powered boom sprayers. The scope of the chemical application needs, efficiency, and economics must be balanced when selecting equipment. No single machine will provide for every need. Several types and sizes of applicators may be necessary for safe, effective, and efficient application of various chemicals.

Hand-Operated, Nonpowered Sprayers

This equipment requires no power source to pressurize the unit. Most of these sprayers described in this section are inexpensive, require minimal maintenance, and are simple to operate.

Hose-end Sprayer. A small container with chemical is attached to a garden hose. The chemical is drawn into the water by venturi action as water passes through the hose end. Hose-end sprayers are suitable for small turf areas, shrubs, and small trees.

Hose-end sprayers naturally require access to a water source. They are suitable for most formulations, but are most effective for materials that are soluble in water. Formulations requiring agitation, such as wettable powders, must be frequently shaken. Hose-ends are not effective or suitable for large areas. They should not be used on tall trees because the sprayer will not operate at near vertical positions. These sprayers are difficult to calibrate, and changes in water pressure will significantly alter output and uniformity. Hose-ends are probably not the best choice for routine pesticide application.

Compressed Air Sprayer. Compressed air sprayers are available as hand-held or back-pack units. These sprayers consist of a small container (1 to 5 gallons in

Compressed air sprayers require frequent pumping (*Figure 60*) to maintain constant pressure. Loss of pressure during spraying significantly alters output. Pressure limiting valves and pressure gauges increase accuracy and reduce pressure fluctuation during operation. Regular maintenance is required for continued operation and to prevent corrosion of metal parts.

Wick Applicators. These specialized applicators deliver postemergent herbicides. The herbicide is gravity fed from a reservoir to a sponge or rope wick (*Figure 61*). The wick is wiped on the weed leaving a thin film of herbicide. Wick applicators are an excellent method for applying non-selective herbicides around or

Figure 59. Backpack compressed air sprayer.

volume) attached to a short hose and spray wand (*Figure 59*). The wand normally contains a single nozzle, but multi-nozzle sprayers are available. Nozzles which adjust from a fine mist to a solid stream are common for homeowners. The unit is pressurized with a hand-operated pump and is capable of developing fairly high pressures.

Compressed air sprayers are suitable for small landscapes, shrubs, and small trees. These small units are especially useful for spot spraying and for areas inaccessible to larger application equipment. The sprayers are suitable for applying most formulations, but those requiring agitation (such as wettable powers) will need frequent shaking.

Figure 60. Hand-operated pump for compressed air sprayer. Frequent pumping is required.

Figure 61. Wick applicator to deliver postemergent herbicides.

under trees and shrubs, where drift to the nontarget plant may be harmful. Wick applicators must be cleaned frequently and used only with water soluble herbicides.

Power Sprayers

Power sprayers require an auxiliary gas, electric, or solar power source to pressurize (a pump) and deliver the liquid. Most power sprayers are equipped with tank agitators (to constantly mix the spray solution) and pressure regulators (to eliminate pressure fluctuations). Many contain elaborate nozzle systems. Power sprayers are relatively expensive and complex depending upon size, accessories, and ultimate use. They require

frequent maintenance, but are a necessity for applying pesticides to large areas.

Low Pressure Sprayers. Low pressure sprayers (10 to 200 psi) are the most common and versatile power sprayers used in landscape application (*Figure 62*). Sprayers may be equipped with a single, hand-held nozzle or have a multi-nozzle boom for rapid application over a wide area. They are used to apply chemicals to turf or trees, and suitable for all pesticide formulations. They also can be easily adapted for liquid fertilizer applications.

High Pressure Hydraulic Sprayers. These sprayers generate relatively high pressures (> 200 psi), are equipped with a single nozzle

Figure 62. Walking boom for a low pressure sprayer.

Figure 63. High pressure sprayer needed for tall trees.

(*Figure 63*), and use all pesticide formulations. High pressure sprayers are essential for pesticide application to tall trees and to penetrate dense foliage. They may be adapted for soil injection of both pesticides and fertilizers.

Controlled Droplet Applicators (CDA). Liquid is precisely metered through a nozzle onto a spinning serrated disk. Centrifugal force throws the liquid out in a very uniform droplet size. Controlled droplet applicators are best suited for herbicide and insecticide applications. These units have a low output and are advantageous where water is limited. Their use in landscape maintenance has been limited, due to expense and maintenance, but technological improvements have increased interest in them.

Sprayer Nozzles

Nozzle selection is one of the most important decisions of chemical application. Nozzle type determines not only the amount of spray applied to a particular area, but also its uniformity, coverage, and the amount of drift. Each nozzle type has specific characteristics and capabilities and is designed for use under certain application conditions. Remember, a single nozzle type and size is not ideal for every situation. The selected nozzle needs to be evaluated for effectiveness, uniformity, and potential drift. *Table 17* can be used for selecting the correct nozzle for an application.

Flat-fan Nozzles. Flat-fan nozzles are used for most broadcast sprays of pesticides and fertilizers. These nozzles produce a flat oval spray pattern with tapered edges. They are available in various standard spray fan angles and are usually spaced 20 to 30 inches apart on the boom at a height of 10 to 30 inches. Recommended boom heights for standard spray angles are shown in *Table 18*.

Standard flat-fan nozzles have a suggested operating pressure from 30 to 60 psi. Extended range flat-fan nozzles operate over a wider range between 15 and 60 psi. The ideal operating pressure for an extended range flat-fan nozzle is between 15 and 30 psi. In this range, the nozzle will produce medium to coarse

189

Table 17. Recommended nozzle types for liquid spray application.

Nozzle type	Herbicides/insecticides /fungicides		Growth regulators
	Contact	Systemic	
Pre-Orifice Flat-Fan		Excellent	Excellent
Extended Range Flat-Fan	Excellent	Good	Excellent
Standard Flat-Fan	Good		Good
Wide-Angle Full Cone		Excellent*	
Wide-Angle Hollow Cone		Good	
Twin Flat-Fan	Excellent*		Good
Turbo-Flooding		Excellent*	Good
Standard Flooding		Fair	

*Except for fungicides

Table 18. Recommended boom height for various spray angles and nozzle spacings.

Nozzle spray angle (degrees)	Boom height for 20-inch spacing (inches)	Boom height for 30-inch spacing (inches)
65	21-23	-NR-
73	20-22	29-31
80	17-19	26-28
110	10-12	14-18

NR - Not recommended if height is above 30 inches.

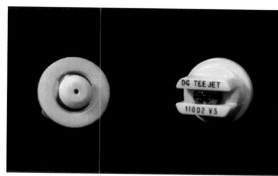

Pre-orifice flat-fan nozzles reduce the volume of driftable droplets.

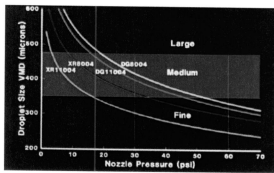

Figure 64. Comparing the mean droplet size of two extended range flat-fans with two pre-orifice flat-fans.

The pre-orifice flat-fan nozzle reduces the volume of driftable droplets under 200 microns by 40 percent when compared to other flat fan nozzles using the volume mean diameter at a pressure of 35 psi. The pre-orifice flat-fan nozzles produce "medium" sized droplets while the same orifice size in the extended-range flat-fan nozzles produce "fine" droplets (*Figure 64*).

The twin flat-fan nozzle design incorporates two flat-fan nozzles — one 30 degrees forward and the other 30 degrees backward — and mounted in one nozzle body. The dual angle improves foliage penetration and spray coverage. Recommended to be used from 30 to 60 psi, the twin flat-fan nozzle produces small droplets for more thorough coverage.

Because the outer edges of the spray patterns of flat-fan nozzles have tapered or reduced volumes, nozzles must be carefully aligned and at the proper height so adjacent patterns along the boom will overlap to obtain uniform

droplets that are less susceptible to drift than finer droplets produced at pressures of 40 psi or greater.

Flat-fan nozzles also are recommended for some foliar-applied herbicides and fungicides at pressures of 40 to 60 psi. These high pressures will generate finer droplets for maximum coverage on the plant surface, significantly increasing the possibility of drift. Appropriate precautions must be taken to minimize drift.

coverage. The most effective pattern is achieved when overlap is 30 to 50 percent of the nozzle spacing. Due to the uniform pattern, when correctly overlapped, the flat-fan nozzle is generally the best choice for the broadcast application of herbicides.

Wide-Angle Full Cone Nozzles. Wide-angle full cone nozzles provide a uniform, circular pattern at pressures from 15 to 40 psi. Droplet sizes are larger than with other nozzle types of the same capacity, making it a good choice to reduce drift. Mount the nozzles at a 45 degree angle and 100 percent overlap for an excellent balance of uniform distribution and drift control.

Wide-Angle Hollow Cone Nozzles. Wide-angle hollow cone nozzles have a large nozzle orifice that reduces clogging and a dual chambered design which produces large droplets. The nozzles produce a circular pattern at pressure ranges from 20 to 50 psi. Nozzles should be mounted like the wide-angled full cone. However, the spray pattern from the wide-angle hollow cone will not be as uniform as a full cone.

Flooding Nozzles. Standard flooding nozzles produce a wide-angle flat-fan pattern and are commonly used for applying fertilizers and mixtures of herbicides and liquid fertilizers. The nozzle spacing on the boom for applying herbicides and fertilizers is generally 40 inches. Flooding nozzles should be operated within pressures from 8 to 25 psi for maximum coverage and drift control. Changes in pressure will affect the width of the spray pattern more with this type of nozzle than with flat-fan nozzles.

The distribution pattern of the standard flooding nozzle is usually not as uniform as a flat-fan nozzle. The most uniform pattern is obtained when flood nozzles are oriented to spray at about 45 degrees above the horizontal and at a height to obtain at least double coverage or 100 percent overlap.

The Turbo-flooding nozzle is constructed with a pre-orifice and a turbulence chamber that produces a flat-fan spray pattern and larger droplets. At common operating pressures, the Turbo-flooding nozzle produces droplets that are 30 to 50 percent larger than those of a standard flooding nozzle. A standard flooding nozzle has heavy edges on the spray pattern and makes a uniform spray pattern difficult to achieve. The Turbo-flooding nozzle reduces the heavy edges and maintains a uniform spray pattern even as the nozzle wears.

Nozzle Materials. Nozzles can be made from several materials. The most common are brass, nylon, thermoplastic, stainless steel, and ceramic. Stainless steel and ceramic orifices will last longer than brass or nylon and will generally produce a more uniform spray pattern over an extended time. Plastic nozzles with stainless steel or ceramic inserts offer an alternative to solid stainless steel nozzles at a reduced cost. Thermoplastic nozzles have good abrasion resistance but swelling can occur with some chemicals and the nozzles are easily damaged when cleaned.

Orifice Size. Since most nozzles are only effective over a limited range of pressures, the proper orifice size is critical. Several nozzle manufacturers provide catalogs that show typical sprayer set-ups and nozzle operating parameters. These catalogs are guidelines to help the operator calibrate and fine-tune the sprayer.

Technology for Improved Spray Accuracy

The pesticide application and turfgrass industries continue to strive for ways to eliminate turf pests while protecting the operators, those in contact with the turf, and the environment. For example, manufacturers use computer technology to calibrate spray equipment, monitor spray coverage rate, and to help make decisions for pesticides, such as when to use or what products and rates would be most effective.

Spray Controllers. Spray controllers compensate for ground speed variations encountered in turf terrain that cause the applicator to speed up or slow down. Most systems monitor travel speed via magnetic sensors or radar devices and measure the flow of spray solutions through an electronic flow sensor. This information is relayed to a microprocessor which automatically regulates a control valve to achieve the desired application volume.

Most spray controllers have boom sections that are

The control console and micro-processor for a spray controller.

individually monitored, so when a section is shut off, the controller automatically compensates to correct the application volume for the remaining sections.

Spray controllers are excellent add-on equipment, but are limited in the range of travel speed variation they can correct for due to the recommended range of nozzle pressures. This means that controllers have limitations and can at times be pressurizing nozzle output to the point that small driftable spray particles become a problem or pressure is too low to achieve sufficient spray pattern.

Direct Injection Systems.
Direct injection systems can give a sprayer infinite rate control. The system uses water or pesticide carrier from the spray tank and the pesticide is metered into the boom at the desired rate depending on speed and other inputs (level of infestations, etc.).

Direct injection systems have several advantages that controllers and manual power sprayers do not. First, the pesticides are not mixed in the spray tank. This eliminates potential exposure of pesticide concentrates at mixing time. However, the greater benefit is that rinsates and leftover tank solution can be practically eliminated.

Other advantages include being able to independently

select a single desired pressure to match the desired droplet size for your spraying needs. Nozzle pressures can be maintained to reduce drift potential and a uniform spray pattern can be maintained.

Since the pesticide formulations are kept in separate containers, the use of closed mixing systems will become standard. Operators may be able to return pesticide material not used during a season, further reducing pesticide storage, inventory, and waste.

Direct injection systems have been under continual investigation. The greatest concern is the accuracy of the metering device. Since pesticide formulations vary greatly with specific density and viscosity, an accuracy metering device is essential. Manufacturers have several methods to assure correct metering. Some calibrate the metering device for each chemical used. Some have identification cards that change the metering device based on pesticide characteristics. Some use a small flow meter that monitors the metering device as a secondary check.

Probably the greatest benefit of these systems lies in the future. As the industry develops sensors that can identify pests and their concentration, a direct injection system can use this information to apply pesticide rates that will effectively control these pests without having to use a broadcast rate for maximum control. Areas with little infestation will not receive pesticides, reducing the amount of pesticides applied. This concept is considered prescription application.

Closed Mixing Systems. Closed mixing systems minimize the amount of exposure to people mixing and transferring pesticides. Most systems are portable units that fit on top of the tank opening or are used with an inductor. These systems allow operators to mix bagged pesticides into a sprayer without opening the bag. When properly used, the system eliminates the possibility of inhaling pesticide dust.

These systems clean 1, 2.5, and 5 gallon containers to triple rinse standards. The empty pesticide container is inserted upside down and the unit spout washes fresh water into the container and residue is deposited in the spray tank.

Sprayer Shields. In searching to find a method to control drift while still providing flexibility when spraying, shielded

booms have become increasingly popular. The shields fit over either mounted or walking booms. When properly adjusted, the shields don't contact the spray, but minimize the effect of wind on the spray pattern, reducing drift potential.

Boom Height Control. Since boom height is critical for spray pattern uniformity, several manufacturers have included manual or automatic adjustable booms. The automatic boom control uses a sonar sensor mounted close to the end of the boom. As the sprayer transverses the surface, a sound wave is emitted and reflected from the turf, telling the sensor how far the boom is from the ground. If adjustments are needed, an electronic screw actuator automatically corrects the boom height.

Chemical inductor for a sprayer to reduce operator exposure to pesticides and to clean empty chemical containers.

Granular Application Equipment

The availability of equipment to apply granular pesticides or fertilizers is less extensive and the machinery is less flexible than that available for liquid materials. Machines constructed of stainless steel, heavy plastic, or other non-corrosive material will provide longer service.

Granular spreaders can be used to broadcast seed. Granular formulations of pesticides are generally safer to use than their liquid counterparts. Granular formulations usually have a low percent of active ingredients, reducing the possibility of serious damage from over-application.

Granular applicators also have several limitations. The volume of the carrier cannot be adjusted as with liquid materials, so each product must be calibrated individually. The actual product must be used during calibration, resulting in potential operator exposure and environmental pollution. Fewer products are available in granular form than in liquid formulations. Some granular products, especially postemergence foliar herbicides, are less effective than their liquid counterparts. Despite the disadvantages, many homeowners and lawn-care services use only granular formulations as a marketing

advantage to counter some neighbor's or client's environmental concern about spray drift.

Hand-Operated Granular Applicators. Hand-operated granular applicators can be carried or strapped to the operator's chest. An adjustable opening at the bottom of the hopper meters the pesticide onto a spinning disk turned by a hand crank. The speed at which the operator turns the crank determines the width of application. These spreaders are relatively inexpensive and easy to use. Calibration is complicated because of operator variation in walking and cranking speeds.

Centrifugal Spreaders. The pesticide is metered onto a spinning disk. When the pesticide strikes the disk, it is thrown by centrifugal force in a relatively uniform pattern around the spreader. The speed of the disk determines the effective spreader width. The disk speed is controlled by ground speed with ground-driven applicators. Some spreaders use an external power source, such as a small electric motor or power take-off (PTO), to drive the disk. These "powered" spreaders are mounted on utility vehicles or tractors and disk speed is independent of ground speed.

Centrifugal spreader powered by a tractor PTO.

Drop Spreaders. Drop spreaders contain a box or hopper mounted between two wheels. As the spreader is pushed, the wheels turn a baffled cylinder within the hopper which meters the granules through adjustable openings at the base of the hopper, allowing the granules to fall on the ground.

The swath width of drop spreaders equals the width of the hopper — usually 3 to 5 feet. Output is controlled by adjusting the size of the opening on the bottom of the hopper and, to a lesser extent, ground speed. Some drop spreaders can be pulled behind a utility vehicle, but most are pushed by the operator.

Drop spreaders are useful for applying granular materials in areas where the swath of a centrifugal spreader is too wide. Drop spreaders have a low coverage per unit of time (low capacity) because of the narrow swath. They are also prone to skips and overlaps of applied materials. The problem of skips and overlaps is reduced by applying half-rates of the material in two, perpendicular applications (*Figure 65*). This method takes twice as long to cover an area.

Air Spreaders. Air spreaders meter granules through an orifice, or with a fluted roller,

Figure 65. Apply half of the chemical over the lawn and apply the other half at right angles to the first pattern to minimize skips and overlaps.

Figure 66. An air spreader.

into a venturi where they are suspended in an airstream and carried through hoses to deflectors mounted on a boom (*Figure 66*). At the deflectors, the granules are distributed in a pattern similar to that of a flat-fan nozzle. When properly calibrated, air spreaders can uniformly distribute materials over a wide range of application rates.

Calibration

Accurate calibration of application equipment is critical for every successful pesticide application. Inaccurate or sloppy calibration has economic, legal, and environmental ramifications. Under-application results in potential poor pesticide efficacy, repeated applications, and reduced profit margin. Over-application increases the possibility of damage to the site, replacement of sensitive landscapes, lawsuits, and is a breach of the Federal Insecticide, Fungicide and Rodenticide Act (FIFRA) Over-application of pesticides can result in

198

civil and criminal penalties.

Calibrating Liquid Application Equipment

Preseason visual checks of a sprayer are not adequate for accurate application, nor is the fact that the equipment and nozzles are new. A Nebraska survey found that only one of six turfgrass sprayers were applying pesticides within five percent of their intended application rate. This survey shows that sprayers must be calibrated frequently to ensure all nozzles have the correct flow rate and are applying pesticides uniformly.

Before calibrating a sprayer, service the entire unit. Check for uniform nozzle output and spray pattern, and determine exactly how much liquid the sprayer tank holds.

Servicing. Clean all lines and strainers, making sure the strainers are in good condition and are the correct size for the type of chemical formulation being applied. Inspect all hoses for signs of aging, damage, or leaks and hose clamps for corrosion. Check the pressure gauge to determine if it is working properly. Does the pressure remain constant and does it read zero when the pump is shut off? The actual accuracy of the gauge is not as important as its ability to give the same pressure reading each time. At least once a year, preferably at the beginning of the spraying season, check the gauge against another gauge which is known to be acc- urate.

Boom pressure may be lower than the pressure at the pump or sprayer manifold. To determine pressure loss, operate the sprayer at a known pressure, then install a gauge on one of the nozzle outlets on the boom and record the lower pressure (*Figure 67*). Check nozzle pressure at several operating pressures to develop a nozzle pressure table. If large variations exist, examine the plumbing system.

Nozzle Output and Spray Pattern. Check for uniformity of nozzle output and for consistency of spray angles, spacing, and height. To check for uniform nozzle output, install the selected nozzles, partially fill the spray tank with clean water, and operate the sprayer at a pressure within the recommended range. Place a container (for example, a quart jar) under each nozzle and check to see whether all the jars fill in about the same time. Inexpensive calibration flow meters are available for direct readings of individual nozzle flow rates as a method to quickly check nozzle output. Replace any nozzles that have an output that varies more than 10 percent from the average of all nozzles, have an obviously different fan angle or distorted spray pattern, or which have an output 10 percent greater than the original nozzle discharge rates.

To determine whether a uniform pattern is being produced and whether the boom is at the proper height, spray some water on a warm dry surface, like a paved road or concrete drive, and watch the drying pattern. If

Figure 67. Spray boom height and operating pressure should be checked at several locations across the boom.

the pattern is not uniform, some strips or areas will dry slower than others. Effective application requires avoiding skips and major overlaps in the spray pattern. Regardless of how much time and effort has gone into calibration and preparation, a non-uniform spray pattern could cause more harm than good.

One method to assure uniform application is to use a spray dye indicator with the tank mixture. This indicator helps the spray operator maintain the proper amount of overlap and detect defective or clogged nozzles. Dye indicators can be an effective additive for hand-held sprayers to aid in obtaining uniform and complete coverage.

Proper swath overlap is easily obtained when the sprayer is equipped with a foam-marking system. They drop foam from the end of the boom, providing a visible cue to the applicator swath. Remember that the distance between the overlapping swaths should equal the distance between nozzles on the boom. For example, if the nozzle spacing is 20 inches, maintain a 20-inch spacing between the end nozzles on successive sprayer passes.

Tank Capacity. It's necessary to know the exact capacity of the spray tank to accurately mix chemicals. Using an inaccurate tank capacity when determining application rates is a common cause of under- and over-application. A tank which is thought to hold 200 gallons, but actually holds 250 gallons, results in a calibration error of 25 percent.

The best and easiest way to accurately determine tank capacity is to fill the tank using any convenient container for which an exact capacity is known. If the container capacity is unknown, fill the container with water and weigh it. Water weighs 8.33 pounds per gallon. Another effective way to measure tank capacity is with an accurate flow meter.

Regardless of the type of equipment used, two pieces of information are necessary to calibrate liquid application

For proper swath overlap use a foam-marking system.

equipment: sprayer output and coverage rate.

Sprayer Output. Sprayer output is usually measured in *fluid ounces per minute* (OPM). Materials needed to measure output are a stopwatch, a container to catch the liquid, and an accurate liquid measuring device calibrated in fluid ounces.

Equip the sprayer with the nozzle or nozzles that will be used in the actual spraying operation. Calibrate the sprayer at the same operating parameters (such as pressure) that will be used. For multi-nozzle boom sprayers, measure the output for each nozzle and then add the amounts together to determine total output.

Operate the sprayer in a stationary position for a pre-determined time (usually less than a minute) and collect the output in the collection containers (*Figure 68*). Measure the amount collected and record the value. Repeat this output measurement at least two more times to accurately determine output. Use the *average* of the three recorded values to determine output in ounces per minute (OPM).

If it is more convenient to work with sprayer output in *gallons per minute*, divide the output in fluid ounces per minute by 128 to determine the output in gallons per minute.

This method for determining output can be used for most sprayers. One exception is high pressure sprayers commonly used for application of pesticides to tall trees. These sprayers deliver a relatively large volume of material under very high pressures. Collecting the output in a container is practically impossible. To determine the output of high pressure sprayers, fill the spray tank with water to a predetermined level and operate the sprayer under actual spray conditions (without fertilizers or pesticides) for a measured time. Record the amount of water (gallons) needed to refill the tank to the original level. Repeat this procedure at least two more times to determine average output.

Figure 68. Nozzle output determination with calibrated containers and stopwatch.

Coverage Rate. The second piece of information required for accurate calibration is *coverage rate* or the amount of time it takes to spray a

Determining Coverage Rate

Materials needed to determine coverage rate are a stopwatch and a tape measure. Measure and mark a known distance between 25 and 100 feet. The calibration distance for self-propelled spreaders should be greater than that used for manual sprayers. Run the sprayer at exactly the same speed to be used on site and record the time it takes to go the measured distance. Repeat this procedure at least two more times to ensure accuracy. Use the average of these three measurements to determine sprayer speed.

Next determine the *effective spray width* of the sprayer. The effective width of a boom sprayer is the product of nozzle spacing and the number of nozzles on the boom. From the time needed to travel the prescribed distance and the effective spray width, the coverage rate is:

Coverage Rate = $\dfrac{\textbf{Time (min)}}{\textbf{\{ Effective Swath Width (ft) X Travel Distance (ft) \}}}$

To determine the coverage rate for a hand-held or hose-end sprayer, measure and mark a known area (i.e. 4 feet by 25 feet) that is typical of the surface to be applied (*Figure 69*). Then measure the time required to cover this area. The coverage rate will depend on the walking speed so be as consistent as possible. The coverage rate is determined by dividing the time (minutes) by the known area (ft^2).

Calibration Calculations

After measuring the total output from the sprayer in fluid ounces per minute or gallons per minute and the coverage rate in min/ac or min/1,000 ft^2, spray volume can be determined by one of the following:

oz/ac	= OPM X min/ac
oz/1,000 ft^2	= OPM X min/1,000 ft^2
GPA	= GPM X min/ac
gal/1,000 ft^2	= GPM X min/1,000 ft^2

Example 1. Suppose a groundskeeper has a power sprayer with 12 nozzles (XR8005) spaced 20 inches apart. Output from each nozzle was collected over 30 seconds. The average of this discharge was 28 ounces (over 30 seconds) or 56 OPM or an equivalent discharge of 0.44 GPM. The individual nozzle discharges were within 10 percent of the boom average (50-62 OPM).

The spray rig was driven over 200 feet at its desired speed setting of 3 mph. It took 45 seconds to cover the 200 feet. The coverage rate was calculated as:

$$\text{Coverage rate} = \frac{45 \text{ seconds} \times \left(\frac{\text{min}}{60 \text{ sec}}\right)}{20 \text{ ft} \times 200 \text{ ft}}$$

$$= 0.000188 \text{ min/ft}^2$$
or
$$= 0.188 \text{ min/1000 ft}^2$$

The spray volume can be calculated as:

$$\text{gal/1000 ft}^2 = 0.44 \text{ GPM} \times 12 \text{ Nozzles} \times 0.188 \text{ min/1000 ft}^2$$
$$= 0.99 \text{ gal/1000 ft}^2$$

or

$$\text{oz/1000 ft}^2 = 56 \text{ OPM} \times 12 \text{ Nozzles} \times 0.188 \text{ min/1000 ft}^2$$
$$= 126 \text{ oz/1000 ft}^2$$

The desired application volume was 1 gal/1000 ft² so this spray unit is ready to go.

Example 2. Suppose an applicator is using a lawn spray gun and has collected 1.3 gallons in a container from the gun over 30 seconds. The spray gun output would be 2.6 GPM.

An area is flagged that is 30 feet by 40 feet and it takes about 30 seconds to make an application to this 1200 ft² area. The coverage rate is:

$$\text{Coverage rate} = \frac{30 \text{ seconds} \times \left(\frac{\text{min}}{60 \text{ sec}}\right)}{30 \text{ ft} \times 40 \text{ ft}}$$

$$= 0.00042 \text{ min/ft}^2$$
or
$$= 0.42 \text{ min/1000 ft}^2$$

The spray volume can be calculated as:

$$\text{gal/1000 ft}^2 = 2.6 \text{ GPM} \times 0.42 \text{ min/1000 ft}^2$$
$$= 1.08 \text{ gal/1000 ft}^2$$

If the desired application volume was 1 gal/1000 ft² the application system would need fine-tuning since the spray volume is outside the ± 5 percent criteria. The pressure could be reduced and adjusted so that the spray gun output is reduced to about 2.4 GPM or the speed of the coverage rate increased so that the coverage rate is reduced to 0.38 min/1000 ft². Adjust and recalibrate.

given area. For most large scale spraying operations this is expressed in *minutes per acre* (min/ac). For smaller applications, it is usually more convenient to express coverage rate in *minutes per 1,000 square feet* (min/1,000 ft²). (See *Determining Coverage Rate* on page 202.)

Some pesticide labels have specific oz/ac, oz/1,000 ft², or GPA requirements. For example, a label may specify, "apply this product with a minimum of 60 gallons of water per acre." If the sprayer, as equipped and calibrated, results in an output that is higher or lower than required for a particular pesticide, it should be adjusted. Reduce sprayer output by: 1) decreasing the nozzle orifice size; 2) decreasing the spray pressure; and/or 3) increasing the sprayer speed. Conversely, sprayer output may be increased by: 1) increasing nozzle orifice size, 2) increasing spray pressure, or 3) decreasing the sprayer speed.

After adjustments are made, recalibrate.

Tank Mixing Pesticides

Once a sprayer has been accurately calibrated, pesticides can be added to the tank (*Figure 70*). This is often when many errors occur. Mismeasured pesticides or

Figure 69. Determining coverage rate of a hand-held or hose-end sprayer.

Figure 70. Correct tank mixing is essential for proper application.

miscalculation of the amount of product to be added can cause gross over- or under-application of pesticides.

Errors are often made when dry ounces are not distinguished from fluid ounces. Remember, to avoid confusion there are *16 dry ounces per pound and 128 fluid ounces per gallon.* Dry ounces are a weight or mass measurement and fluid ounces are a volumetric measurement. Containers used to measure fluid ounces are never appropriate for measuring dry weights. Keeping these simple, but often overlooked, points clear is paramount to accurately adding pesticides to a spray tank.

Product labels normally list rates in the amount of *product* required for a given area or application. Universities and federal and state agencies, however, often express recommendations on an *active ingredient* (AI) basis. Because pesticides are rarely formulated as 100 percent active ingredient, the amount of product and amount of AI are not synonymous. For example, to apply a 50W product at a rate of 1 pound AI per acre, it is necessary to apply 2 pounds of product per acre since 1 pound of 50W product contains 0.5 pounds of AI. If the operator had applied only 1 pound of product per acre, the pesticide would have been inadvertently under-applied.

Make sure, when adding a pesticide to a spray tank, that the *desired rate* and *amount added to the tank* are equivalent.

Spray Techniques

Be aware of the proper application procedures and consistently follow them. There are also differences in procedures among the various types of equipment.

Power Sprayers. Boom sprayers have good control and provide uniformity and accuracy of application. Follow the proper procedures to minimize over-application while improving efficacy.

The first step is to survey the area to be sprayed. Look for obstacles and sloping or rough terrain. If moveable objects are in the way, remove them. It is best to spray parallel to the length of the field, starting against a square end if possible. Doing so will minimize turning and on/off time. This also allows for more uniform application. Do not spray while turning. Instead, spray the ends (headers) of the turf area after completing the area. If the headers are sprayed first, the applicator will be driving through wet foliage. In some cases, traffic can cause turfgrass phytotoxicity from accumulated herbicides on the sprayer's tires.

Sprayer speed directly influences application rate. Doubling the travel speed cuts the application rate in half and traveling at half the desired speed doubles the application rate. An accurate speedometer or monitor can help maintain a constant speed.

Monitor the spray pressure to ensure that the sprayer is operating as determined during calibration. Periodically inspect the spray pattern, looking for leaks, plugged nozzles, and proper tank agitation.

Hand-Held Applicators. Hand-held applicators are available in a wide range of lances and nozzles to accommodate different applications. Most single nozzle units are equipped with a multi-purpose nozzle that can be adjusted to produce a cone pattern with a fine spray to a coarse stream. This nozzle is useful for spot treating individual weeds or trees, but it is not effective for large areas.

Most prefer an even flat-fan nozzle for spraying large areas. The application volume can be varied by selecting a different size of orifice with a known output. When spraying, maintain a constant pressure in the tank and hold the nozzle stationary at the proper height. The fan pattern should be perpendicular to the direction of travel. Waving a flat-fan nozzle wand back and forth will result in non-uniform coverage.

Hand-guns require considerable operator skill to evenly spray large areas. Proper delivery and uniform coverage are dependent on walking speed and gun motion. Gun motion consists of waving the gun in a back-and-forth, side-to-side motion. Hold the gun at any angle from 45 degrees to nearly parallel to the ground. The speed at which one walks will influence the gun motion.

Use a gun motion that will hit a target two or three times with the spray pattern while moving forward. Establish a consistent walking speed that allows for gun motion and reduces fatigue. A good training method to attain a proper gun motion is to practice on a paved area using water in the sprayer and then watch the drying patterns.

Calibrating Granular Application Equipment

Chemical manufacturers may provide information for settings on granular applicators, but these should be used only as starting points. Manufacturers are as precise as possible with calibration guidelines, but several variables must be measured for accurate calibration.

Variables affecting granular application rates are ground speed, swath width, and meter opening. Ground speed with hand-pushed spreaders will vary with the operator, so each operator should calibrate the spreader accordingly.

Swath width depends on the type of spreader, and uniform application of the pesticide is dependent on the operator's ability to maintain proper overlap between swaths. The meter opening is adjusted to distribute a certain amount of pesticide for a given speed and swath width. It cannot be accurately set if the operator does not maintain a nearly constant ground speed and swath width. Since different granules have different flow characteristics, applicators must be calibrated for each material.

Calibrating granular application equipment is similar to the process described for liquid applicators, but with several subtle differences. The carrier (water) volume for liquid applicators can be increased or reduced depending on the particular operation. A granular pesticide concentration is fixed and cannot be adjusted because it is typically formulated with an inert carrier. This requires calibration for every granular product used. Also, the actual pesticide (or fertilizer) must be used during calibration since the size and density of

granular products vary. Relative humidity also can affect granule flow so applicators should be recalibrated under extreme conditions of humidity.

The first step in calibrating a granular applicator is to calculate the area to be covered (coverage rate). For drop spreaders, coverage is simply the width of the hopper multiplied by a distance. For example, coverage area of a drop spreader with a 4-foot wide hopper traveling 25 feet is 100 square feet (4 feet x 25 feet = 100 square feet).

The swath width of a centrifugal spreader is controlled by the speed of the centrifugal disk. It can be altered by cranking speed of hand-cranked spreaders, ground speed of ground-driven spreaders, or rotational speed for powered spreaders. Swath width and coverage rate by these spreaders is variable and must be determined for the speed used in actual pesticide applications.

To determine the swath of centrifugal spreaders, lay a row of collection vessels on a one-foot spacing perpendicular to the spreader's line of travel (*Figure 71*). The containers can be cigar boxes, pie tins, or similar receptacles. Each container should have the same dimensions. Load the spreader with the pesticide to be applied and set the opening on a medium setting.

Figure 71. To make a quick check, lay out a row of shallow cardboard boxes at a right angle to the direction of travel.

at which to operate the spreader, calibrate the machine at the recommended setting, collect and weigh the output, and adjust the settings as necessary.

Drop Spreader. Output from drop spreaders can be collected in one of two ways. Most commercial drop spreaders come with a **calibration pan**. This is attached beneath the spreader to collect output when the spreader is pushed over the calibration course. If a calibration pan was not included with the spreader, a catch pan can be fabricated. Other calibration methods include pushing the spreader over a concrete surface or trap and measuring the discharge. However, when a spreader is pushed along a surface dissimilar to landscape, large differences in wheel speed could result in inaccurate application. Using a calibration pan is more efficient and the spreader can be calibrated on the actual surface to be treated.

Run the spreader at the speed to be used in actual operation over the collection containers. This operation should be done at the shop or in an open or paved area, **not** on the lawn or driveway. Check the collection containers for granules. By observing the amount and distribution of the material in the collection containers, spreader swath can be reasonably estimated. If the material in each container is weighed, distribution and application rate can be checked and adjusted.

The final step in calibrating a granular applicator is to determine the spreader setting required to apply the amount of material, based on the determined rate coverage, to equal the desired rate. To determine the **correct** setting

If the initial setting does not deliver the desired amount, adjust it. If the collected amount is less than the calculated requirement, increase the setting or decrease travel speed. Conversely, to lower output decrease the output setting or increase applicator speed. Once a setting is found which delivers the desired amount, collect output at least two more times and average the results to ensure accuracy.

Centrifugal Spreaders. Using a calibration pan with centrifugal spreaders is impractical. The normal procedure for collecting output from a centrifugal application is to operate the spreader over a tarp or plastic sheet of known dimensions. Weigh the output. The expected volume for the size of the catch tarp must be calculated. If the tarp is wider than the spreader swath, then coverage is simply calculated as swath width multiplied by tarp length. If the tarp is narrower than the spreader swath, then coverage rate is equal to the catch tarp area. If the initial setting does not deliver the desired amount, then appropriate adjustments will be needed.

Because the speed of travel of ground-driven centrifugal spreaders affects spreader swath, increasing or decreasing speed will affect coverage rate. Adjusting the speed of the applicator cannot, therefore, be used to alter output for a ground-driven spreader.

Adjusting travel speed can alter output for mounted, powered centrifugal spreaders or any centrifugal spreader whose disk speed is independent of ground speed.

Operators should remember that it is extremely difficult, if not impossible, to calibrate a granular spreader to deliver **exactly** the desired amount. Granular pesticides contain low concentrations of the active ingredient to help compensate for inherent calibration inaccuracy. The operator should adjust the settings so that delivery is as close as reasonably possible to the recommended amount. The operator, however, should and must be willing to settle for close. If the desired amount is within 10 percent of the calculated amount, the applicator should proceed with the application confident that the granular material is being applied in a safe and effective manner. To help ensure uniform distribution of granular applicators, some operators divide the rate by two, then use double coverage. This means applying one-half of the material in one direction and the other half in a direction perpendicular to the first (*Figure 65*). When this method is used, the granular spreader must be calibrated to apply one-half the desired rate.

Looking Ahead

Application equipment for the future will provide for increased operator safety, precise application, and protection of the environment. Invest in the future by updating your application equipment and conducting regular maintenance and calibration checks.

By keeping your equipment in good working condition and practicing appropriate pesticide safety and management strategies, you demonstrate your sensitivity to individual workers and the environment. Be a beacon of responsibility.

Pesticide Laws, Regulations, and Guidelines

Larry D. Schulze
Extension Pesticide Coordinator

- Federal regulations
- Pesticide classifications
- Developing and registering pesticides
- Certifying applicators
- Label information
- Applicator liability
- Protective clothing
- Pesticide use guidelines

esticide development, registration, and use are tightly regulated by federal and state laws and regulations to ensure that pesticide products are beneficial, effective, and have minimal risk to users, the public, and the environment. From the point of view of the pesticide user, the pesticide label is the most prominent evidence of these requirements. The label assures that regulatory requirements have been met and guides product use so that people and the environment are protected.

Federal Pesticide Law

Pesticide laws and regulations have been adopted to protect people and the environment. The Federal Insecticide, Fungicide and Rodenticide Act (FIFRA) was first enacted in 1947 and has been amended several times. FIFRA has specific provisions on pesticide registration, classification, labeling, distribution, use, and other topics.

FIFRA is administered and enforced by the U.S. Environmental Protection Agency (EPA) through a lead agency in each state. Usually, the state department of agriculture or its equivalent is the lead agency. All pesticide products sold in the United States must be approved in advance by

EPA after a review of the manufacturer's application for registration, the intended pesticide label, and related data. Pesticides are approved by the EPA only if they are shown to be effective and not present an unreasonable risk to people or the environment.

The process that leads from a newly synthesized chemical in the laboratory to an EPA-approved pesticide available for marketing is detailed, expensive, and time-consuming. Pesticide products are subject to at least 120 tests in order to receive and maintain EPA product label registration. The exact group of tests that must be performed for each pesticide depends on how it will be used. For example, a pesticide that would not be used on food or feed crops would not require extensive residue and metabolism tests.

A summary of tests performed by a manufacturer for submission to the EPA for consideration of an approved label includes product chemistry, physical/chemical characteristics, wildlife impact, toxicology, plant protection, re-entry studies, non-target insect impact, environmental fate, residual chemistry and efficacy, and spray drift.

The pesticide developmental process leading to an EPA approval commonly takes eight to ten years and can cost over $50 million. This process assures pesticide applicators and the public that the product may be safely used and that the quality of the environment is maintained.

One of the fundamental guidelines to assure that people and the environment are protected is through the proper use and application of the pesticide. In all cases, a pesticide may only be legally applied to an approved site listed on the label. This site may be a crop, a location, an animal, or a structure.

When an application is made to the labeled site, this action assures pesticide safety to the applicator, for the consumer, for wildlife, and for the environment. Supplemental laws and regulations as enacted by states can further limit pesticide use within that state's borders.

Classification of Pesticides

All pesticides are classified by the EPA according to use:

1. General use pesticides; and
2. Restricted use pesticides.

A general use pesticide can be purchased and used by the general public without undue hazard to the applicator or the environment as long as the label instructions are carefully followed. Most pesticides are classified as general use.

A restricted use pesticide (RUP) is available for pur-chase and use only by certified pesticide applicators or persons under their direct supervision.

Pesticides are classified as restricted use for a variety of reasons, including the product's toxicity and its potential to injure people, the type of formulation, the method and use of the pesticide, its intended site or place of use, and its potential hazard to wildlife or the environment.

FIFRA includes record-keeping requirements for certified applicators using restricted use pesticides. Individual states may add additional reporting requirements. Typical recordkeeping requirements for a commercial applicator may include:

1. Name and address of the person for whom the pesticide was applied;
2. Name, address, and certified applicator number of person making the application;
3. Location of pesticide application;
4. The target pest;
5. Site of application, i.e., crop, commodity, location;
6. Date and time of application;
7. Trade name and EPA registration number of pesticide applied;
8. Amount and rate of pesticide applied; and

9. Type and amount of pesticide disposal, method of disposal, date of disposal, and location of disposal site.

FIFRA regulations require that these records be retained for two years, but state requirements may be stricter. Nebraska, for example, requires these records to be kept for three years for both general and restricted use pesticides when commercially applied to turfgrass.

Private applicators also may be required to keep records of their restricted use pesticide applications. Such is the case with the 1990 Farm Bill. The pesticide use records for private applicators are similar to those required for commercial applicators. Some states also may require other pesticide records for private applicators or general use pesticides.

Classification of Applicators

Only those persons who are certified may buy, apply, use, or supervise the use of restricted use pesticides. Under the FIFRA guidelines, there are two types of certified pesticide applicators: private and commercial.

A private applicator is a certified applicator who uses or supervises the use of any restricted use pesticide for producing agricultural commodities on property owned or rented by him/her. This includes farmers, vegetable growers, and hired farm laborers. A private applicator may apply restricted use pesticides without compensation by trading personal services between producers of agricultural commodities.

A commercial applicator is a certified applicator who uses or supervises the use of any restricted use pesticide on any property not owned or rented by him/her. This includes persons applying any restricted use pesticides as employees or for hire. Some state regulations provide additional categories of pesticide applicators. Examples are registered technicians or non-commercial applicators. Some states require certification for the commercial application of general use pesticides.

FIFRA and the individual states provide specific training and testing requirements for these categories of applicators. FIFRA and state regulations also provide specific guidelines for the recertification of certified applicators.

Pesticide Registrations

The three types of pesticide registrations are federal, special local needs, and emergency exemption. Most pesticides are registered under federal registrations (a Section 3 registration). Once the EPA registers a pesticide, the resultant label is assigned an EPA registration number. This number is unique to that particular active ingredient or combination of active ingredients, their concentration, the pesticide formulation, and its intended use.

Special local needs (SLN) registrations provide an option for individual states. Under FIFRA, a state may register additional uses for a federally registered pesticide if certain requirements and conditions are met. Typically, an SLN registration adds additional application sites or control techniques to those already listed on the federal label. The SLN is sometimes known as a Section 24(c) registration.

When a state approves an SLN registration, supplemental pesticide labeling must be provided. Pesticide applicators must have a copy of the SLN supplemental registration in their possession in addition to the federal registration to apply the pesticide for that additional use. An SLN registration is legal only in the state or area specified in the labeling for the given time.

The third type of pesticide registration is the emergency exemption from registration. It is commonly known as a Section 18 registration. In some cases when an emergency pest situation develops for which no pesticide is registered, an emergency registration can be used. These registrations are typically approved by the state lead agency, usually a state governor or a federal agency head. An emergency exemption allows a pesticide product to be sold and used for a nonregistered purpose for a specific time. There are very strict controls and recordkeeping requirements for Section 18 pesticides.

In all pesticide applications, applicators must be aware of their specific responsibilities and requirements.

Pesticide Residues and Tolerances

The EPA's approval of the pesticide product and its subsequent use according to the approved label are assurances that the pesticide's active ingredients will not present an unnecessary risk to people and the environment. Under this approach, minute quantities of synthetic pesticides are allowed on agricultural commodities intended for food or feed. The pesticide quantity which remains in or on food or feed is called a residue. Pesticide residues are allowed up to a given point. The EPA sets pesticide tolerances as a maximum amount of pesticide residue which may remain on or in treated crops and animals that are sold for food or feed.

Pesticide tolerances are determined through intensive testing and research to assure consumer safety. Typically, the pesticide tolerance is set at least 100 times lower than the amount known to be hazardous. Food or feed products may not be distributed, sold, or marketed if a pesticide residue exceeds the pesticide tolerance.

Liability of Pesticide Usage

Pesticide applicators have legal responsibilities for their actions associated with the use and application of a pesticide. Typically, if an individual applied a general use pesticide, the liability of such use rests on the applicator.

When restricted use pesticides are applied, the liability for these products rests on the certified applicator. If guidelines allow an uncertified applicator to apply a restricted use pesticide under the supervision of a certified applicator, the liability rests with the certified applicator.

For these reasons, all pesticide applications should be applied as directed by the pesticide label.

The Pesticide Label

The pesticide label is the legal document that provides the requirements and guidelines associated with the product's use. Information on the specific use of a pesticide formulation is provided through labels and labeling. While the words are similar, they have distinctly different meanings.

The pesticide label is the pertinent information on or attached to the pesticide container. The label contains specific information of interest to pesticide users.

Labeling includes the label itself, plus all other information received from the manufacturer about the product, including booklets, brochures, flyers, and other information. Labeling also may include information provided by the EPA concerning endangered species and their habitats and worker protection standards.

It's important to understand an underlying principle associated with pesticide application methods. Essentially, any method of pesticide application is allowed if not specifically prohibited by the label. An example would be the use of a broadleaf weed herbicide on turfgrasses. Unless specifically prohibited by the label, the product could be applied by a tractor-mounted sprayer, by a hand-wand from a supply tank, by a hand-pump sprayer, or by the use of a paint brush and can. All of these application methods are legal means of applying the material to turfgrasses if not specifically prohibited by the label.

Major Components of the Pesticide Label

The manufacturer is required by law to furnish certain information on the pesticide label. Pesticide label requirements include:

1. *Brand, trade, or product name.* A specific brand name, usually registered as a trademark, will identify a product as produced by a specific manufacturer.

2. *Ingredient statement.* Every pesticide product label must have the active and inert ingredient amounts (percentage by weight) printed on the label. The active ingredients must be identified.

3. *Manufacturer.* The name and address of the manufacturer, registrant, or formulator who makes the product must be printed on the label.

4. *EPA registration number.* An EPA registration number is assigned, indicating the label was approved by the EPA before sale in the marketplace.

5. *EPA establishment number.* An establishment number identifies the specific facility where the product was formulated.

6. *Classification statement.* All pesticides are classified on the basis of hazards, intended use, and effect upon the environment. Pesticide use is classified either for "general use" or "restricted use." Training and certification is required for an applicator to buy, apply, or supervise the application of a "restricted use" pesticide.

7. *Directions for use.* The instructions for applying the pesticide are most important. They include the application rate, the site it is intended to protect, the pest controlled, mixing instructions, and other related information.

8. *Signal words and symbol.* A signal word — DANGER, WARNING, or CAUTION— must appear in large letters on the front panel of the pesticide label. A signal word indicates how acutely toxic the product is to humans. The signal word is based not only on the active ingredient, but on the toxicity of the formulated product. The skull and crossbones symbol and the word "POISON" are required on labels of pesticides that are highly toxic and are likely to cause acute illness through oral, dermal, or inhalation exposure. Products that have the signal word "DANGER" due only to skin and/or eye irritation potential, will not carry the word "POISON" or the skull and crossbones symbol.

9. *Precautionary statements (protective clothing and equipment).* These statements guide the applicator to take proper precautions to protect humans

217

or animals that could be exposed. A "route of entry" statement suggests the route(s) most likely for a specific product to enter a person and suggests specific actions to prevent exposure. The protective clothing requirements statement provides requirements and/or guidelines specifying the correct type(s) of protective equipment that should be used when handling the material.

10. *Statement of practical treatment.* First aid treatment guidelines are recommended in this statement in case of overexposure.

11. *Environmental hazard statement.* This statement includes requirements and common sense reminders to avoid contamination of the environment, including air, water, soil, and wildlife exposure.

12. *Reentry statement.* This statement indicates how much time must pass before a person can reenter a treated area without appropriate protective clothing. It is commonly referred to as the "restricted entry interval."

13. *Storage and disposal statement.* The storage of the pesticide and the disposal of the empty container are important responsibilities of the applicator. Use the best storage and disposal guidelines for the specific situation and location.

14. *Worker Protection Standard.* The EPA issued the Worker Protection Standard (WPS) to protect employees on farms and in forests, nurseries, and greenhouses from exposure to agricultural pesticides (general or restricted use). Sod farms and operations that produce plants (flowering and foliage plants or trees, tree seedlings, live Christmas trees, vegetable, fruit, and ornamental transplants) for subsequent transplanting to another location are covered by the Worker Protection Standard. See the EPA manual, *The Worker Protection Standard for Agricultural Pesticides - How to Comply*, for more information.

The pesticide label is recognized as more than just a piece of paper with guidelines. Courts of law also recognize it as a legal document. It is the applicator's responsibility to follow the requirements as listed on the pesticide label and labeling.

Environmental and Applicator Protection Emphasis

In recent years, pesticide labels have placed greater emphasis on protecting the applicator and environment. Specific guidance about using the pesticide product helps provide for maximum protection for the applicator, water, soil, and wildlife resources. State laws may provide additional requirements such as antipollution devices if the pesticide is applied through chemigation.

Proper rinsing of liquid pesticide containers is required. This may be accomplished through triple rinsing or pressure rinsing. Rinse the pesticide container immediately upon emptying. The most convenient method of rinsate disposal is to add the rinse water to the spray tank and use it to dilute the pesticide mixture. Always apply the rinsate to the labeled site as identified on the label.

Some specific directions for the use of the pesticide product are only referred to in the pesticide labeling. It is the responsibility of the pesticide user to obtain and follow product labeling in these situations.

Additional requirements which may be listed in the labeling include endangered species protection requirements; pesticide transportation, storage and disposal; and worker protection standard requirements.

The labeling statements for the endangered species protection program will refer the pesticide user to a pesticide use county bulletin. These bulletins provide pesticide product restrictions in certain areas of a county for the protection of endangered or threatened species.

Protective Clothing and Equipment

There are three means by which a pesticide can enter the human body: oral (through the mouth), dermal (through the skin or eyes), and by inhalation (breathing into the lungs). The type of protective clothing and equipment needed depends on the toxicity of the pesticide, the type of formulation, and the potential route of exposure to the applicator's body.

The applicator is legally responsible to follow all guidelines for personal protective clothing and/or equipment listed on the label or labeling. These requirements have become stricter with the implementation of the Worker Protection Standard.

Typically, skin and eye exposure is most common while using and handling pesticides. It is also the easiest route of entry to prevent. Chemical-resistant gloves that cover the hand and forearm provide excellent protection. Unlined gloves made of nitrile, neoprene, or butyl rubber are excellent choices. Some labels on fumigant pesticides will guide the user not to wear gloves because the gloves can trap the fumigant gas near the skin and cause injury. The label will be the specific guide.

Pesticides often are spilled or splashed onto the body during the mixing and measuring operations. Personal protective equipment and clothing requirements are often different during mixing/loading operations than for the pesticide application.

The label may require eye protection, such as goggles. Goggles are designed to fit comfortably over glasses, have shielded vents and prevent splash into the sensitive eyes.

Appropriate footwear is commonly overlooked when handling pesticides. Leather or fabric shoes can easily absorb pesticide products. Special care must be taken so that these materials do not absorb pesticides. Chemical-resistant boots or shoe coverings should be worn when required.

Proper laundering of pesticide contaminated clothing is essential for applicator safety. Always wash pesticide contaminated clothing immediately after use and separate from other laundry. When washing pesticide-contaminated clothing, prerinse, use hot water and a heavy duty liquid detergent, and use the maximum water level. When the washing cycle is completed, run the washer through a complete cycle without clothing but with detergent to clean the machine.

Good personal hygiene while working with pesticides is very important. Applicators can reduce any potential risks associated with pesticides by using the proper protective clothing/equipment and proper washing of pesticide contaminated clothing. If an applicator suspects that he/she was exposed to a pesticide that could be poisonous, be aware of signs and symptoms of pesticide exposure and take appropriate medical action.

Pesticide Development

The development of a pesticide is expensive, lengthy, and arduous. It may take eight to ten years for an active ingredient synthesized in a laboratory to become available on the market.

After a new active ingredient is developed in a laboratory, it is tested in a variety of ways. There are laboratory, greenhouse, and field tests to determine how effectively the pesticide controls the target pest. If the new compound shows merit as a potential pesticide because of its ability to control target pests, numerous other studies are initiated. These studies cover the product's toxicology, degradation, product residue in food and feed, impact on wildlife and the environment, and potential market opportunities. The manufacturer submits the information to the EPA for review and approval before sale in the marketplace. Upon approval, the pesticide label receives an EPA registration number.

There are approximately 700 active ingredients that make up about 20,000 pesticide products in the United States. Active ingredients may be sold under several formulations.

Pesticide Use Guidelines

Pesticide Spray Drift

Spray drift away from the intended target is an important and costly problem in residential settings. Drift lowers the amount applied to the target area which reduces effectiveness, and can damage off-target sites, resulting in environmental contamination.

Drift occurs by two means: vapor drift and particle drift. Vapor drift occurs when fumes from the evaporating pesticide, after application, moves with the wind to nontarget sites. Particle drift is the actual movement of small spray particles away from the target area.

Several factors affect spray drift, but the most important is the size of the spray droplet. Small droplets fall through the air slowly and are carried further by air movement. Whenever possible during application, keep the pressure of the pesticide solution as low

as practical. Droplet size is then larger and less susceptible to drift. Shields are often used to reduce spray drift from nozzles.

Be aware of excessive winds that can cause a pesticide loss from the target area to nontarget sites. Most recommendations are to stop spraying if wind speeds are over ten miles per hour or when adjacent to sensitive plants.

In all cases, read and follow the pesticide label to insure the safe and effective use of the pesticide with minimal risk to the environment.

Transportation

The careful transport of pesticides from one location to another is important. Protect the pesticide container from any damage. Secure pesticide containers to prevent tipping or puncture. Transport a pesticide in the bed of a truck or in the trunk of a car. Do not transport a pesticide in the passenger compartment.

Posting of Treated Areas

Some states require the posting or placarding of pesticide treated areas in residential lawn environments. Check for specific state and local requirements that may affect your applications.

Figure 72 provides a sample flag design that may be adapted as needed. Space is

Figure 72. Sample posting flag for lawn pesticide applications.

sometimes provided on the flag to write what product was applied and the date of application.

Reentry Statements

Some pesticide products will have caution statements about entering a treated area after an application. The reentry statement shows you how much time must pass before individuals can enter a treated area without appropriate protective clothing.

If the pesticide that has been applied has no reentry statement on the label and your state has no local requirements, then general guidelines are that liquid sprays should be allowed to dry and dust or granular products must settle before entering a treated area without protective clothing.

Pesticide Storage

Pesticides should be stored to prevent access by children, pets, or unauthorized persons. Storage should be secure, preferably locked, and out of sight.

Pesticides are required to be kept in the original containers with a label attached. Never temporarily store a pesticide in an unmarked container.

Pesticide Safety Telephone Hotline Numbers

Recommendations and guidance in regard to pesticide safety are available through several toll-free telephone numbers. The National Pesticide Telecommunications Network [800-858-7378] is an excellent resource for medical and consumer information on pesticides. The Chemical Referral Center [800-262-8200] can refer you to the manufacturer of any pesticide product. The Center can provide name, address, and phone number of a registrant's headquarters.

An emergency number associated with pesticides is The Poison Center [800-955-9119] based at Children's Memorial Hospital in Omaha. This facility supports telephone calls originating from Nebraska and adjoining states. Be aware of the telephone number of the closest Poison Center that can be of assistance to you. (*See Inside Back Cover.*)

The Pesticide Accident Hotline [800-424-9300] is also known as CHEMTREC. Through this hotline from the Chemical Manufacturers Association, one can receive immediate guidance during emergencies involving a pesticide spill or leak. This center can provide information on how to contain a spill, clean it up, and properly dispose of it.

Contact the State Patrol Office in your state or other appropriate authority to report chemical spills or releases. This is the same number to use to report motor vehicle accidents on public roadways.

Read and Follow the Pesticide Label

Consider the pesticide label as the source of guidelines and requirements for activities related to that product. It is important to read and follow the pesticide label:

• **Before buying.** Read the label to determine which product is best for your need. Always buy pesticides in small quantities so they may be used in a relatively short time.

• **Before mixing and using.** Review the protective clothing/equipment requirements on the label before opening and measuring the pesticide material. Determine the rate, measure accurately, and calibrate application equipment.

• **Before storing.** The label will provide guidance on proper storage of the pesticide product. It is wise to prevent the pesticide container from contacting moisture and to prevent liquid formulations from freezing. Because some pesticides contain petroleum distillates, pesticide storage should be away from open flame. Always store pesticides in the original container in a secure place away from children, animals, and unauthorized persons.

223

- **Before disposal.** Rinse the empty pesticide container and use the rinse water to dilute the spray mixture. Read the label for guidelines on disposing of surplus pesticides. Use community hazardous waste collection programs, if available. A pesticide application according to the label is the best method of use **and** disposal.

Additional Sources
of Information

- Publications
- Periodicals
- Biological supplies
- Insect monitoring devices
- Extension pesticide information offices
- Pesticide control officials
- Pesticide resources

Publications

Turfgrass Management

Beard, J.B. 1982. *Turf Management for Golf Courses*. Burgess Publishing Company. Minneapolis, Minnesota.

Decker, H.F. and J.M. Decker. 1988. *Lawn Care: A Handbook for Professionals*. Prentice-Hall. Englewood Cliffs, NJ.

Schurtleff, M.C., T.W. Fermanian and R. Randell. 1987. *Controlling Turfgrass Pests*. Prentice-Hall, NY.

Turgeon, A.J. 1991. *Turfgrass Management*. Prentice-Hall. Englewood Cliffs, NJ.

Watschke, T.L., P.H. Dernoeden and D.J. Shetlar. 1995. *Managing Turfgrass Pests*. Lewis Publishers, Boca Raton, Ann Arbor, London, Tokoyo.

World Wide Web/Internet Sites. To electronically access publications related to the topics in this book, see the Resources site under Extension publications on the University of Nebraska Institute of Agriculture and Natural Resources home page: http://ianrwww.unl.edu/ianr/pubs/catalog/home.htm. It offers a vareity of state and national publications dealing with related subjects.

For more information on pesticides, see the Pesticide Education Resources home page, University of Nebraska, Lincoln, http://ianrwww.unl.edu/ianr/pat/ephome.html.

For more information on biological control methods, see the Midwest Biological Control News Home Page at http://www.wisc.edu/entomology/mbcn/mbcn.html.

Weed Identification and Management

Anderson, W.P. 1996. *Weed Science: Principles and Applications*. West Publishing, St. Paul, MN.

Gaussoin, R.E. and R. C. Shearman. 1992. *Lawn Weeds and Their Control*. North Central Regional Extension Publication No. 26. University of Nebraska, Lincoln, NE.

Turgeon, A.J. 1994. *Turf Weeds and Their Control*. American Society of Agronomy. Madison, WI.

Weeds of the North Central States. North Central Regional Publication No. 281. Bulletin 772. University of Illinois at Urbana-Champaign, IL.

Whitson, T.D. et al. 1991. *Weeds of the West*. Western Society of Weed Science and the University of Wyoming.

Insect Identification, Biology, and Management

Audubon Society Field Guides, *Insects and Spiders*, Alfred A. Knopf, New York, NY.

Baker, J.R., ed. 1982. *Insects and Other Pests Associated with Turf, Some Important, Common and Potential Pests in the Southeastern United States.* North Carolina Agricultural Extension Service.

Baxendale, F.P. and R.J. Wright. 1996. *Insect Pest Management Strategies for Yards and Gardens.* Extension Circular EC96-1555. Cooperative Extension, University of Nebraska, Lincoln, NE.

Davidson, R.H. and W.F. Lyon. 1987. *Insect Pests of Farm, Garden and Orchard*, 8th Ed., Wiley and Sons, New York, NY.

Golden Guides: *Insects and Insect Pests*, Golden Press, Western Publishing Co., Racine, WI.

Johnson, S. V. 1988. *Nebraska Insects*, 2nd Ed. Nebraska Dept. of Agriculture, Lincoln, NE.

Niemczyk, N.D. 1981. *Destructive Turf Insects.* HDN Book Sales. Wooster, OH.

Peterson Field Guides: *Insects*, Houghton Mifflin, Boston, MA.

Simon and Schuster Field Guides: *Insects*, Simon and Schuster, New York, NY.

Shetlar, D.J., P.R. Heller and P.D. Irish. 1990. *Turfgrass Insect and Mite Manual.* 3rd Ed. Pennsylvania Turfgrass Council.

Tashiro, H. 1987. *Turfgrass Insects of the United States and Canada.* Cornell University Press, Ithaca, NY.

Disease Biology and Identification

Couch, H.B. 1995. *Diseases of Turfgrasses.* Krieger Publishing Co., Malabar, FL.

Leslie, A. R. 1994. *Integrated Pest Management for Turf and Ornamentals.* Lewis Publishers, Boca Raton, FL.

Shurtleff, M.C., T.W. Fermanian and R. Randell. 1987. *Controlling Turfgrass Pests,* Prentice-Hall, Englewood Cliffs, NJ.

Smiley, R.W., P.H. Dernoeden and B. B. Clarke. 1992. *Compendium of Turfgrass Diseases.* APS Press, St. Paul, MN.

Smith, J.D., N. Jackson and A.R. Woohouse. 1989. *Fungal Diseases of Amenity Turf Grass.* E and F.N. Spon, New York.

227

Vargas, J.M., Jr. 1994. *Management of Turfgrass Diseases,* 2nd Ed. Lewis Publishers, Boca Raton, FL.

Watschke, T.L., P.H. Dernoeden and D.J. Shetlar. 1995. *Managing Turfgrass Pests.* Lewis Publishers, Boca Raton, FL.

Pesticide Use and Application

For the latest information on pest management and pesticides in your state, contact your local Extension office.

Bohmont, B. L. *The Standard Pesticide User's Guide.* 1990. Prentice-Hall, Englewood Cliffs, NJ.

Environmental Protection Agency. 1993. *The Worker Protection Standard for Agricultural Pesticides — How to Comply.* U.S. EPA, Washington, D.C.

Laughlin, J. and R. E. Gold. 1989. *Laundering Pesticide Contaminated Clothing.* NebGuide G89-943. Cooperative Extension, University of Nebraska, Lincoln, NE.

Ogg, C. L. and L.D. Schulze. 1994. *Worker Protection Standard for Agricultural Pesticides.* NebGuide G94-1219. Cooperative Extension, University of Nebraska, Lincoln, NE.

Ogg, C. L. and L. D. Schulze. 1993. *Protective Clothing and Equipment for Pesticide Applicators.* NebGuide G94-758. Cooperative Extension, University of Nebraska, Lincoln, NE.

Schulze, L. D. and E. F. Vitzthum. 1984. *Signs and Symptoms of Pesticide Poisoning.* NebGuide G84-715. Cooperative Extension, University of Nebraska, Lincoln, NE.

Schulze, L. D., R. Grisso and R. Stougaard. 1990. *Spray Drift of Pesticides.* NebGuide G90-1001. Cooperative Extension, University of Nebraska, Lincoln, NE.

Schulze, L. D. and S. T. Kamble. *The Pesticide Label.* 1989. NebGuide G89-937. Cooperative Extension University of Nebraska, Lincoln, NE.

Title 40, Code of Federal Regulations, Part 156: "Labeling Requirements for Pesticides and Devices." U.S. Government Printing Office.

U.S. Environmental Protection Agency and U.S. Extension Service. *Applying Pesticides Correctly – A Guide for Private and Commercial Applicators.* 1991. U. S. Department of Agriculture.

Vitzthum, E. F. and L. D. Schulze. *Pesticide Laws and Regulations*. NebGuide G79-479, rev. Cooperative Extension, University of Nebraska, Lincoln, NE.

Watschke, T.L., P.H. Dernoeden and D.J. Shetlar. 1995. *Managing Turfgrass Pests*. Lewis Publishers, Baca Raton, FL.

Pesticide Application Efficiency

Agnew, M.L. and N.E. Christians. 1990. "The mathematics of turfgrass maintenance." GCSAA.

Bohmont, B. L. *The Standard Pesticide User's Guide*. Revised 1990. Prentice-Hall, Englewood Cliffs, NJ.

Couch, H.B. 1995. "Relationship between nozzle type, pressure at the nozzle, and fungicide effectiveness and procedures for making accurate and uniform fungicide applications" IN: *Diseases of Turfgrass,* 3rd Ed. Krieger Publishing Co. Malabar, FL.

Grisso, R.D., D.L. Varner, and R.N. Klein. 1991. *Plumbing Systems of Agricultural Sprayers*. NebGuide G91-1020. Cooperative Extension, University of Nebraska, Lincoln, NE.

Grisso, R.D. and R.N. Klein. 1988. *Fine Tuning a Sprayer with the "Ounce" Calibration Method*. NebGuide G88-865. Cooperative Extension, University of Nebraska, Lincoln, NE.

Trusty, S. and S. Trusty. *"Fertilizer spreader selection: choice distribution."* SportsTurf, August 1993.

Varner, D.L., R.D. Grisso and R.C. Shearman. 1990. "Calibration accuracy of golf course pesticide applicators." *Applied Engineering in Agriculture* 6(4):405-41.

Way, T.R., K. Von Bargen, R.D. Grisso and L.L. Bashford. 1990. "Chemical flow control systems for injection-type sprayers." *SAE Transactions, Journal of Commercial Vehicles* 99(2):340-349.

Way, T.R., K. Von Bargen, R.D. Grisso and L.L. Bashford. 1993. "Feedback system to control chemical flow for injection sprayers." *Computers and Electronics in Agriculture* 9(2):123-132.

Wildlife Management

Hygnstrom, S.E., R.M. Timm and G.E. Larson. 1994. *Prevention and Control of Wildlife Damage.* Cooperative Extension, University of Nebraska, Lincoln, NE.

Abiotic Damage

Danneberger, T.K. 1993. *Turfgrass Ecology and Management.* Franzak and Foster G.I.E. Inc., Cleveland, OH.

Bennett, W.F. 1993. *Nutrient Deficiencies and Toxicities in Crop Plants.* APS Press, St. Paul, MN.

Periodicals

Golf Course Management, 1421 Research Park Drive, Lawrence, KS 66049-3859.

Grounds Maintenance, P.O. Box 12901, Overland Park, KS 66282-2901.

Landscape & Irrigation, P.O. Box 10514, Riverton, NJ 08076-0514.

Landscape Management, 1 East First St., Duluth, MN 55802.

SportsTurf, 68-860 Perez Road, Suite J, Cathedral City, CA 92234.

IPM Practitioner: Common Sense Pest Control Quarterly, Bio-Integral Resource Center, P.O. Box 7414, Berkeley, CA 94707.

Biological Supplies

Ward's Natural Science Establishment, Inc.
5100 West Henrietta Road
P.O. Box 92912
Rochester, NY 14692-9012
(800) 962-2600

Carolina Biological Supply Co.
2700 York Road
Burlington, NC 27215
(800) 334-5551

BioQuip Products
17803 LaSalle Ave.
Gardena, CA 90248
(213)324-0620

Forestry Supplies, Inc.
205 W. Rankin Street
P.O. Box 8397
Jackson, MS 39284-8397
(800) 647-5368

A.H. Hummert Seed Co.
2746 Chonteau Ave
St. Louis, MO 63107
(800) 325-3055

Insect Monitoring Devices, Other IPM Supplies

Great Lakes IPM
10220 Church Road NE
Vestaburg, MI 48891
(517) 268-5693

Pest Management Supply Co., Inc.
P.O. Box 938
Amherst, MA 01004
(413) 243-3747

Extension Pesticide Education Offices

The following offices provide educational opportunities and training and can direct you to other resources in your state.

Colorado
Colorado State University
Department of Soil and
Crop Sciences
Fort Collins, CO 80523
(303) 491-6027

Iowa
Iowa State University
Department of Entomology
Insectary Building
Ames, IA 50011-3140
(515) 294-1101

Kansas
Kansas State University
Department of Entomology
Waters Hall
Manhattan, KS 66506
(913) 532-5891

Minnesota
University of Minnesota
Plant Pathology Department
495 Borlaug Hall
1991 Buford Circle
St. Paul, MN 55108
(612) 624-3477

Nebraska
University of Nebraska
101 Natural Resources Hall
Lincoln, NE 68583-0818
(402) 472-1632

North Dakota
North Dakota State
University
NDSU Pesticide Programs
P.O. Box 5658
Fargo, ND 58105
(701) 231-7180

South Dakota
South Dakota State
University
Agriculture Hall, 237
Box 2207A
Brookings, SD 57007
(605) 688-4752

Wyoming
University of Wyoming
Plant, Soil and Insect
Science Department
College of Agriculture
Box 3354
University Station
Laramie, WY 82070-3354

Pesticide Control Officials

For specific pesticide information pertinent to your state, contact the appropriate office listed below:

Colorado
Colorado Department of
Agriculture
Division of Plant Industry
Pesticide Section
700 Kipling Street, Suite
4000
Lakewood, CO 80215-5894
(303) 239-4139

Iowa

Iowa Department of
Agriculture
Pesticide Bureau
Wallace Building
Des Moines, IA 50319
(515) 281-8591

Kansas

Kansas Department of
Agriculture
Plant Health Division
Pesticide Registration
Section
901 S. Kansas Street
Topeka, KS 66612-1281
(913) 296-2263

Minnesota

Minnesota Department of
Agriculture
Agronomy Services Division
Environmental Regulatory
Section
90 West Plato Blvd.
St. Paul, MN 55107
(612) 296-8547

Nebraska

Nebraska Department of
Agriculture
Bureau of Plant Industry
301 Centennial Mall North
Lincoln, NE 68509
(402) 471-2394

North Dakota

North Dakota Department
of Agriculture
Pesticide Division
600 E. Blvd., 6th Floor
Bismarck, ND 58505-0020
(701) 328-4756

South Dakota

South Dakota Department
of Agriculture
Division of Agricultural
Services
Certification/Registration
Foss Building, 523 East
Capitol
Pierre, SD 57501-3182
(605) 773-3724

Wyoming

Wyoming Department of
Agriculture
Technical Services
2219 Carey Avenue
Cheyenne, WY 82002-0100
(307) 777-6590

Pesticide Resources

Chemical Referral Center
(800) 262-8200

Provides information on
any pesticide manufacturer,
including name, address, and
phone number of a regis-
trant's headquarters.

Pesticide Accident Hotline
(800) 424-9300

Through its hotline, the
Chemical Manufacturers
Association (CHEMTREC),
provides immediate guidance
during emergencies involving
a pesticide leak or spill.

Index

235

Notes

Notes

Integrated Turfgrass Management for the Northern Great Plains

To obtain additional copies of this publication, contact any Nebraska Extension office or use the form below to order directly.

Order form

_____ Enclosed is $32.50 for the handbook, *Integrated Turfgrass Management for the Northern Great Plains*, (shipping and handling included).

_____ Please send me a free catalogue of University of Nebraska Extension publications.

_____ Please send me information on discounts for ordering multiple copies.

Send your check or money order made out to the **University of Nebraska** along with the form below, to:

> Publications
> University of Nebraska
> P.O. Box 830918
> Lincoln, NE 68583-0918

Fill out this section to use a credit card:

Visa _____   Mastercard _____

Credit Card Number _____

Expiration Date _____

Signature _____

Please ship to:

Name _____

Company Name _____

Street Address _____

City _____

State _____

Zip _____

Phone   (   ) _____